PRAISE FOR <u>YOU NEED FRIENDS</u>

"This book beats the drum that we need to hear: God made us for friendship. In our modern moment, there may be no more important message."

– Justin Whitmel Earley,
Business Lawyer and Author of *Made for People*,
Habits of the Household, and *The Common Rule*

"In an age of isolation and loneliness, this simple read points us to the ancient practice of spiritual friendship in a format that works for this generation. Birthed out of the intersection of deep study, a local faith community, and personal experience, Thurston provides a hopeful path forward for the lonely, longing heart."

– Rev. Dr. Andrea Summers,
Campus Pastor and Dean of Spiritual Formation
of Indiana Wesleyan University

"This work by Jake Thurston proclaims one of the most important truths related to human flourishing: you need friends! Friendship with God, self, and others is what you will be reminded of and challenged with in this thorough discourse. In fact, while reading it, I was reminded of the most used two-word phrase in all the Bible related to human existence: 'one another.' Beyond the fact that these two words appear in Scripture around eighty times, we were made by a triune God who lives and leads in relationship. You and I are created for relationship. This is one area in which Christ followers and the church of Jesus should excel—providing the opportunity to offer genuine friendship with God as well as with others."

– Dr. Jim Dunn,
President of Oklahoma Wesleyan University

"You could wade through countless studies that trace how relational behavior has evolved through developments in architecture, sociology, commerce, and technology. You could gain a comprehensive picture of the neuroscience behind loneliness and the research that reveals the negative implications of loneliness on human biology. Or . . . you could read Jake's book that describes all this in a friendly, conversational way. And that's just part one! Jake doesn't leave us hanging. He has also done research into the theology of relational connection, and we now receive the benefit. He lays out a simple pathway that is the culmination of the multidisciplinary approach to address loneliness. Best of all, the action steps are natural, easy, and comfortable. Give your body, mind, and soul the gift of *You Need Friends*."

– Dr. Dave Bushnell,
Founder of Mobilize Leadership

"*You Need Friends* is a timely and heartfelt invitation to rediscover the spiritual richness of life lived in authentic relationships. In a world increasingly marked by isolation, this book reminds us God designed us for connection and community. Through biblical insights, real-life stories, and practical steps, Dr. Jake Thurston beautifully illuminates how friendships are not just optional but essential to our spiritual and emotional well-being. *You Need Friends* is a road map for cultivating relationships that honor God and bring healing to the soul. If you've ever struggled with loneliness or felt disconnected from God, this book will inspire you to embrace the abundant, friend-filled life God intends for you. I wholeheartedly recommend it to anyone longing to deepen their relationships and live more fully in God's plan for community."

– Dr. Ed Love,
Executive Director of Church Multiplication
and Discipleship for The Wesleyan Church

"As soon as I wasn't surrounded by school classrooms and activities, finding 'my people' became more difficult. My desire for friendships didn't change, but they didn't come about as conveniently as the playground days. Jake's book, *You Need Friends*, is the book your soul knows you need. I highly recommend it—may it be the catalyst for you to defeat loneliness and build life-giving community."

– David Kinnan,
Lead Pastor of Fountain Springs Church

"This book is a profound presentation of the reality and power of relationships and the relational God behind them. It will challenge you to not just *do* relationships but to actually *be* relational with the world around you. Dr. Thurston gives language to what every church and church small group strives for but far too many are missing. The Scriptures call it *koinonia*, but Dr. Thurston sums it up ever more clearly: you need friends."

– Phill Tague,
Lead Pastor of Ransom Church

"Ever since I first met Jake, it was clear that he had a word for the church—and this book is it. He has been warning about the increasingly disastrous effects of loneliness in our culture for years. That's why this book is more than just a writing project. It is the result of hard-earned wisdom that only comes from living out the words that he writes here. In this book, Jake clearly and decisively exposes the silent epidemic of loneliness and points to a way forward that every church and ministry leader should attend to. It's time to get back to spiritual friendship!"

– Phil Wiseman,
Lead Pastor of Table Church

For more information, email jake@youneedfriends.com

eBook ISBN: 979-8-89694-132-3
Paperback ISBN: 979-8-89694-133-0
Hardcover ISBN: 979-8-89694-134-7

Reclaim Your God-Given Design for Community &
Remedy Your Loneliness for Good

YOU NEED FRIENDS

JAKE THURSTON

Dedicated to Kasey Jean,
my dearest spiritual friend.

CONTENTS

INTRODUCTION

I had reached my breaking point.

Every day bore a newfound heaviness that was unfamiliar to me. I've always had anxious tendencies, ever since I was a kid, overly stressing about things that didn't need worrying over—storms, grades, social status, *girls*. But I had never felt anxiety to this extent.

This anxiety was different. Deeper. *Crippling.* I felt irritable. I was easily angered, getting flustered over the smallest things. I couldn't produce anything near to the level of what I had accomplished just a month earlier. I had pressing deadlines, massive goals, urgent tasks, and a running to-do list. Yet I couldn't seem to muster the energy, let alone the desire, to do any of it. Which, naturally, produced a rush of guilt and shame that I wasn't producing enough. I'm not contributing enough. I'm slacking. I'm not working forty-plus hours. No matter how hard I tried, I just ran into this wall of anxiety, apathy, lethargy, and depression.

I had never been depressed before. I've obviously been sad and certainly upset, but *this* emotion was entirely new to me. It felt like a ton of bricks welled up inside my chest weighing me down right where I was seated, unable to move, unable to work, unable to feel what I needed to feel. I was, in a word, helpless. I cried into my wife's shoulders that night.

I had *really* reached my breaking point.

Some quick facts about me. I'm an Enneagram type 3. I'm an ENFJ Myers-Briggs personality type. I'm an *I* on the DISC test. Includer,

Positivity, Woo, Communication, and Connectedness are my top five strengths on StrengthsFinder. All that to say, I'm an optimistic, extroverted productivity machine who thrives off being in large crowds and spewing positivity to everyone around me, reminding them of their potential and how they belong, and my first response to any negative emotion is to bury it or run away to other pleasurable things, like Chipotle, coffee shops, or quality time with friends.

So you can probably imagine what social distancing and stay-at-home orders did to me during the initial COVID-19 outbreak in the spring of 2020. It was by far the worst season of my life.

After a lot of processing, journaling, listening to podcasts, and FaceTime calls with friends, I was reminded that my depression, anxiety, irritability, slowness, and lack of productivity were not just trauma responses to a global pandemic.

They were side effects of loneliness.

And millions of people were unknowingly suffering from the loneliness epidemic in our country well before the COVID-19 pandemic.[1]

According to a 2022 study by CIGNA, over half (58 percent) of US adults are considered lonely. This was fairly consistent with the 61 percent of US adults experiencing loneliness in 2019.[2] This percentage tripled the mere 20 percent of Americans who felt lonely forty years ago.[3] Needless to say, loneliness was already at epidemic levels well before the stay-at-home orders and social distancing mandates of 2020.

Additionally, the 2022 CIGNA article reported that

- One in four Americans (27 percent) rarely or never feel as though there are people who really understand them.
- Two in five Americans (43 percent) sometimes or always feel that their relationships are not meaningful and that they are isolated from others.

- One in five people report they rarely or never feel close to people (20 percent) or feel like there are people they can talk to (18 percent).
- Minorities are more likely to experience loneliness: 75 percent of Hispanic adults and 68 percent of Black/African American adults. This is over ten points higher than the 58 percent of the general adult population.
- In comparison to the 55 percent of nonparents who feel lonely, 65 percent of parents and guardians reported feeling lonely.
- Two out of five senior adults (41 percent) aged sixty-six and older report feelings of being lonely.
- And perhaps most surprisingly, four out of five young adults (79 percent) between the ages of eighteen and twenty-four are lonely, making Gen Z our nation's loneliest generation.

The vast amount of people in our country—192 million people—suffer from loneliness on a regular basis. What's most unfortunate is how a lonely life goes against everything of what it means to be human. It increases anxiety, depression, irritability, addictions, physical illness, and chances of early death—not to mention the fact that it makes life seem a little less worth living.

So these questions remain: How did we get here? Why are we so lonely? What is this epidemic doing to us physically, mentally, emotionally, and spiritually? How do we *remedy* such extensive loneliness? And most importantly, how can we reclaim our God-given design for community?

That's what this book is about.

LET ME INTRODUCE MYSELF

My name is Jake. I'm a local church pastor, theologian, husband, and a dad of three kids and one cat. But I am also a friend. For as long as I can remember, God has hardwired me to bring people together, befriend the lonely, and include in activities others who would otherwise be labeled as "outcasts." I *live* for friendship. So when I discovered, while working on my master's degree in 2015, that the United States is in a loneliness epidemic, I was floored. How could this possibly be the case? Additionally, it was right around the same time I learned about a long-lost Christian practice called "spiritual friendship" according to a twelfth-century monk named Aelred of Rievaulx. His treatise articulates a form of earthly friendship that is truly breathtaking when it's redeemed by the gospel of Jesus. So I had a crazy thought:

How could the rediscovery of spiritual friendship remedy our loneliness epidemic?

That sounded like a pretty good master's thesis to me. However, little did I know that this topic would become a ten-year-long research project. In 2017 I wrote my master's thesis about spiritual friendship and the loneliness epidemic. Since then, I've taught classes and workshops and delivered keynote presentations and sermons about this topic. I wrote blogs on my website and was interviewed on podcasts about this topic. I even received my doctorate of ministry (DMin) in August 2024 after studying how the practice of spiritual friendship could decrease feelings of loneliness and increase feelings of social support among thirty participants between the ages of eighteen and twenty-four. The results were astounding.

I say all this to show how passionate I am about this topic. I'm convinced a part of the reason God has put me on this earth is to help people grow in friendship with others and rid themselves of loneliness. This book you have before you is the culmination of a decade's worth of work from my lectures, sermons, blogs, papers, research, studies, ministry, and real-life experience all surrounding the loneliness epidemic and spiritual friendship. If you read this and put its content into practice, I can guarantee you'll reclaim your God-given design for community and remedy your loneliness for good.

So here's where we're heading.

THE JOURNEY BEFORE US

Part 1 takes a deep dive into the loneliness epidemic. In chapter 1, I will show you how it's not good to be alone. Extended periods of loneliness wreak havoc on our minds, bodies, and souls in ways we never could have imagined. It's a silent disease that's lurking beneath so many of our society's problems, more than we realize. However, loneliness is so devastating because we were never meant to be alone. So in chapter 2, I will you show you how God designed you for community. What's just as startling as all the negative effects of loneliness are all the positive effects friendship and community bring to our lives.

Unfortunately, it's very hard to live out our God-given design for community in our culture. In chapters 3 and 4, I will talk about two prominent cultural phenomena—individualism and isolationism, respectively—and how they greatly hinder our ability to connect with others in meaningful community. Remedying our loneliness will require massive effort on our part to push back against the isolating forces of our culture.

But it's way more doable than you think.

In part 2, I will introduce to you the long-lost Christian practice of spiritual friendship as a solution to our loneliness epidemic. In chapter 5, I will show you how vital it is to begin with the most important person we can befriend—Jesus Christ himself. With Jesus as our template for approaching our friendships, chapter 6 will reveal to us the formative power of our earthly friends and their impact on our ability to live out Christ's way of life. Chapter 7, then, will give you practical tips on what types of individuals to befriend who will satisfy your God-given design for community and who will also best form you into Christ's likeness.

One of the best places to find those spiritual friendships, though, is in the local church. In chapter 8, I will show you how it was Jesus's original vision for the church to be a community of friends who function like surrogate brothers and sisters, and why involvement in a local church is so vital. But mere church attendance isn't enough. In chapter 9, I will show you how important it is to dig deeply into the most vulnerable parts of our lives with friends, for doing so will cultivate the close friendships that can yield deep relational satisfaction. Finally, in chapter 10, I will present a framework for how you can regularly meet with a small group of your friends in a way that will draw you deeper into relationship with one another, increase your social support, and decrease your loneliness.

WHO THIS BOOK IS FOR

This book is written for anyone who wants to be rid of their loneliness and grow in satisfying friendships with others at the soul level. Now, I will add that I am a pastor of a Christian church. I profess Jesus as Lord, and I believe that he died, rose again, and will return to restore heaven and earth. I reference the Bible throughout, use Jesus as the template for friendship, and discuss spiritual friendship according to church history. But although I'm writing from a Christian perspective, that does not at all rule out your ability to glean wisdom and practical tips for your life if you ascribe to a different belief system. We all need friends, regardless of who we are and what we believe.

Second, a particular audience I'm writing this book for is Gen Zers and young adults. That's any young adult born between the mid- to late-1990s and the early 2010s, or today's 14-to-27-year-olds.[4] If you can recall from the stats, *four out of five young adults between the ages of 18 and 24 are lonely.* While there is a loneliness epidemic affecting people from all generations, it is particularly prevalent among young adults due to a number of factors unique to their upbringing in our digital, post-Christian culture. However, even if you're not a member of Gen Z, I promise you will still find this book valuable for your journey.

Lastly, I'm writing this book for pastors. I believe the local church bears the hope of the world: the good news of Jesus. But as you'll read, salvation isn't just personal deliverance from sin; it's also adoption into a family. The church should be the greatest friend group to which people can belong. So to my fellow pastors, and especially youth and young adult pastors, this book will reveal the psychology behind the relationships we work so hard to develop in our people, as well as practices to help them cultivate deep, meaningful friendships that inform their spiritual formation.

HOW TO READ THIS BOOK

It only makes sense to read a book about friendship with friends. Read it as a book study with your small group at church, invite a couple of your friends to read it together (book clubs are still cool!), or FaceTime with your best friend from high school. Even if you do read it by yourself, I encourage you to find time to wrestle somehow with its contents with others.

Since I highly recommend reading this book in community, at the end of every chapter are a set of discussion questions for you and your friends to process together. In addition, I implore you to mark up this book with a highlighter or pen, write in the margins, and scribble thoughts in the extra space at the end of chapters, all so you can better cite the points speaking to your soul (and the points you vehemently disagree with!) when you discuss it with your friends. I especially hope that pages accidentally get bent from throwing it in your backpack or purse too quickly—not because I find an odd pleasure in the destruction of books but because you had to pack it up to head over to your friend's house or coffee shop to talk about it.

SO WHAT ARE YOU WAITING FOR?

Perhaps there is no better time for a book like this to arrive than now. People are literally living their worst lives because of prolonged periods of loneliness. Maybe you even find yourself in a similar place of desperation.

So why wait?

It's time to rediscover your God-given need for friendship and find those friends you've been looking for.

PART I

THE LONELINESS EPIDEMIC

CHAPTER 1

IT'S NOT GOOD TO BE ALONE

It is not good for the man to be alone.

– Genesis 2:18 –

You don't have any friends.

(Or at least imagine you don't.)

What would a friendless life be like? Doubtless, you would find yourself at the very least exceptionally bored. While some may enjoy the thought of always being to oneself 24/7, I suspect that even those people would realize they can only take so much of themselves for so long.

Think about it. You wouldn't have anyone to celebrate your birthday with, or to vent to about your hard day at work, or to embark on a late-night Taco Bell run with. You wouldn't have anyone to work out with, laugh with, travel with, play with, cry with. And you certainly wouldn't have anyone who sees you, hugs you, knows you, hears you, and *gets* you.

The longer time persists without such a fundamental relationship that is so surprisingly intrinsic to the human experience, the emptier you begin to feel. The quest for significance would become shockingly dim. A yearning to be known, seen, touched, loved—a desperation to belong—rises to the surface that you never realized was there before. This yearning for connection with other people screams from every fiber of your being, anatomy, biology, psychology—even your soul—longing for someone to reach out, know your name, look you in the eye, and notice you.

Befriend you.

Such a desperation for friends would push you to your limits, whether you realize it or not. The ache of loneliness can reach to the very depths of your soul, disrupting your sense of self-worth, your trust toward good people, and your discipline to abstain from destructive habits. Such a desperation for friends could turn you into an unpleasant person who, ironically, no one else would want to befriend, leaving you alone in a vicious cycle of anxiety, while scanning your environment for possible social "threats."

So much of the joys of this life stem from our friends. Almost everything good in our lives is enhanced by the presence of friends. Playing Kan Jam on a summer evening, going on a four-mile run, worshipping in church, serving the community, reading a fantasy novel, or eating a Chipotle burrito bowl are all life-giving activities in themselves. But they are significantly better when we can do them alongside friends, who bring joy, laughter, and support while we live this life.

But if you lived a friendless life, you wouldn't have any of that. No one to enjoy the simple things with, let alone support you. Simply put, a friendless life goes against everything about what it means to be human. It's a life *no one* wants to live. Why?

Because God designed us never to do this life alone.

THE FIRST PROBLEM

In Genesis 1, God creates the cosmos. He creates the heavens and the earth; the sky, the ocean, and land; the creatures of the earth, sea, and air; and he deems everything as "good." But creation climaxes at the formation of humankind, which God deems "very good"—the crown jewel, the big kahuna, the magnum opus, the most prized possession of everything he created. However, Genesis 2 zooms in on the intricate details of the creation of humanity. And it all begins with a man named Adam:

> When the LORD God made the earth and the heavens, neither wild plants nor grains were growing on the earth. For the LORD God had not yet sent rain to water the earth, and there were no people to cultivate the soil. Instead, springs came up from the ground and watered all the land. Then the LORD God formed the man from the dust of the ground. He breathed the breath of life into the man's nostrils, and the man became a living person. . . .
>
> The LORD God placed the man in the Garden of Eden to tend and watch over it. But the LORD God warned him, "You may freely eat the fruit of every tree in the garden—except the tree of the knowledge of good and evil. If you eat its fruit, you are sure to die." (Genesis 2:4–7, 15–17)

Could you imagine being the first human ever created? Adam was made *directly* by God from the dust of the ground. Fun fact: the Hebrew word *adam* literally means "the man," which stems from the Hebrew word *adamah* for "ground." So, *Adam* could literally mean "the man formed from the ground." In this way, Adam was given exceptional access to his Creator. He was given a job to tend to the garden of Eden, and he was able to do pretty much anything he wanted. Sin hadn't even come into the picture yet. The only rule he had to live by was not to eat the fruit from these two trees in the middle of the garden. Boom. Easy. Talk about paradise, right? As long as you don't mind gardening and being surrounded by animals, I think all of us would have loved to be in Adam's shoes.

But would we really?

Check out what happens next in verse 18: "Then the LORD God said, 'It is not good for the man to be alone'" (Genesis 2:18).

Whoa, whoa, whoa. Hold on. Just in the previous chapter, we saw the full account of God creating the universe. He created the heavens and the earth, light, the sun and moon, the sky, the waters of the deep, the plants, the fish of the sea, the birds of the air, the beasts of the ground, and he called them all *good*. And when he created humanity, he called them *very good*! But it's here, in verse 18, we see God label the very first thing that *wasn't* good.

If you're familiar with the creation story, you might have thought the first problem God had to solve for humanity was sin—our fallen desire to disobey God and pursue our own ways. But that doesn't occur until Genesis 3. No, the first problem God had to solve for humanity was *loneliness*. Here's what happens next with verse 18 in its full context:

> Then the LORD God said, "It is not good for the man to be alone. I will make a helper who is just right for him." So the LORD God formed from the ground all the wild animals and all the birds of the sky. He brought them to the man to see what he would call them, and the man chose a name for each one. He gave names to all the livestock, all the birds of the sky, and all the wild animals. But still there was no helper just right for him. (Genesis 2:18–20)

So, God set out to cure his loneliness by making him a *helper*. And you might be thinking, "A helper? God wants to cure Adam's loneliness by giving him a personal servant?" No, no, no. The word *helper* in verse 18 means so much more than your virtual assistant on your smartphone that helps you calculate your tip at Applebee's or looks up the actress who plays El in *Stranger Things*. "Helper" comes from the Hebrew word *ezer*, which literally means "rescuer," "ally," or "hero." This word is used in the Psalms to describe the kind of aid God provides in battle and great times of need. Some examples of an ezer would be like the Rohirrim showing up to aid Gondor at the battle for Middle Earth, or the Millennium Falcon swooping in to take out Darth Vader and the two TIE fighters, granting Luke Skywalker a clear shot to blow up the Death Star, or all of the Avengers showing up through portals to defeat Thanos.

That's the kind of companion God wants to make for Adam to rid him of his loneliness for good.

But what's fascinating is in Genesis 2, we see the events of Genesis 1 *reversed*. Genesis 1 climaxes with the creation of humanity, as if it were the grand finale of the fireworks show on the Fourth of July at Mount Rushmore. Genesis 2, on the other hand, starts with the creation of humanity, and it is Adam's *loneliness* that triggers God to create the rest of living organisms as candidates for Adam's *ezer*. So God brings up all these animals to Adam and assigns him the job of naming them all in the hope that his interactions with them would lead him to finding his ally, his rescuer, his "war hero."

But it is all to no avail. After naming *every single animal*, verse 20 says, "But still there was no helper just right for him."

That leaves me scratching my head. Why would God go through the trouble of creating all these animals to remedy Adam of his loneliness, only for it all to fall short? Not to mention, why would God even allow for something as bad as loneliness to exist in his perfect creation in the first place?

Despite its lack of goodness, loneliness existed before the fall precisely *because* Adam was made perfect—albeit incomplete. Tim Keller, a renowned pastor and theologian from New York City, once noted in a sermon,

> Adam was not lonely because he was imperfect, but because he was perfect. The ache for friends is the one ache that is not the result of sin. . . . This is one ache that is part of his perfection. . . . God made us in such a way that we cannot enjoy paradise without friends. God made us in such a way that we cannot enjoy our joy without human friends. Adam had a perfect quiet time [with the Lord] every day, 24 hours. He never had a dry [day], and yet he needed friends.[5]

Loneliness, according to the creation account, isn't isolation *from* friendship but an invitation *into* friendship. This parade of animals wasn't a failure on God's part in providing Adam an adequate ezer. God knew what he was doing. God exposed Adam to all these animals so he could so strongly feel his God-given design for communion with someone like him.

Loneliness was God's way of wiring Adam with a physiological reminder that he needed friends.

If Adam was given one rule not to eat from the fruit of the Tree of Knowledge of Good and Evil, that meant he *was* allowed to eat from everything else. Therefore, God would have created Adam with the ability to experience hunger and thirst, which are the body's physiological signals that inform us it's time to eat and drink. As it turns out, loneliness is a physiological trait that God designed us to have as a reminder that we need friends. John Cacioppo, a leading scientist on loneliness, claims loneliness is the "check engine" light for our need for social connection.[6] When viewed this way, loneliness can be an incredibly helpful tool that reminds us to connect with friends, just as hunger and thirst remind us we need to eat food (Chipotle burrito bowls are preferable) and drink water (or GT's Peach Paradise kombucha in particular).

However, if you're like me, as soon as I see any warning lights pop up on my car's dashboard, I immediately question if they're legit. "Oh, my 'check engine' light is on? Eh, it's running fine," I muse. "Surely it's the warning system that's wrong. So I'm just going to keep trucking along and see what happens."

Until one day my engine suddenly explodes.

But it wasn't all of a sudden. I just deliberately ignored all the warning signs until my engine couldn't handle it anymore. It was entirely on me for letting my engine deteriorate to that extent, all because I didn't want to go through the hassle of setting up an appointment at my local mechanic to get it looked at.

Just as our cars deteriorate the longer we ignore the "check engine" light, and just as our bodies become malnourished when we don't eat or drink, so goes our well-being when we snooze—and ignore—our loneliness alarms.

God said it's *not good* to be alone for a reason. And that's not just what the Bible says. It's what science says as well.

THE LETHALITY OF LONELINESS

In its simplest form, loneliness is the subjective feeling of being alone. It can result from extended periods of physical isolation with no one to talk to or connect with, like being the only one working from the office one day a week or being forced to stay at home during a pandemic. However, loneliness is more than just being physically isolated by oneself. People can be by themselves and not feel lonely, while others can be surrounded by people and yet feel very lonely.

That's why loneliness is more about the distress we feel when our ideal relational desires don't align with our perceived relational realities.[7] Sort of like looking for a set of ezers but coming up short.

Loneliness can occur in three different dimensions.[8] The first dimension is intimate, or emotional, loneliness. This occurs when someone longs for an intimate partner, such as a boyfriend, girlfriend, or spouse, or a deeply trusted confidant, like close friends with whom you can share all your deepest struggles. I experienced intimate loneliness pretty seriously throughout high school and college. Despite having a great group of friends, I couldn't shake how desperately I wanted a girlfriend (and having attended a private Christian university, the pressure to find a spouse before you graduate was high—for whatever reason).

The second dimension is relational loneliness, which occurs from a general lack of quality friendships, companionships, and social support. These are friends who know you and want to be with you, where you can embark on wild adventures together while making memories that last a lifetime, or where you're able to have a playdate with your kids while you as moms can catch up. However, these aren't just people with whom you have a good time; they *support* you. They are there for you during your hardest seasons. They build you up when you feel torn down. They mourn with you, they celebrate with you, and they aren't afraid of your mess. But relational loneliness ensues when you perceive this dynamic of friendship is lacking in your life in any way, and not necessarily when you don't have any friends. You could belong to a group of friends and still feel lonely due to a perceived lack of support from each other.

Collective loneliness—the third dimension—is the lack of a larger network or community with others with a shared sense of purpose, passions, and interests. This is a higher form of loneliness we typically don't think about. However, just as we can be disconnected from a group of friends, we can also be disconnected from pursuing a cause or passion that's bigger than ourselves. You could experience collective loneliness when you're working in a job that doesn't seem like it's making a difference in the world or when you're just coasting through life without pursuing something with a meaningful purpose. We yearn to be connected to greater causes, and that's why it's so powerful to belong to teams, communities, networks, workplaces, and organizations that serve these higher purposes. If you're missing out on that, you could be experiencing collective loneliness.

These three dimensions exhibit the full range of social connections we need to feel relationally satisfied and connected. If any one of these dimensions is lacking, feelings of loneliness can ensue. So even if you work for a great cause and have a wonderful marriage, for example, you could still experience relational loneliness because you don't have a group of friends to hang with and support you. But here is the real kicker: loneliness is *subjective*. There is no standard number of friendships one must have in order to not feel lonely. An individual's subjective perception of his or her relationships determines if they are satisfying or lacking. For example, my wife, Kasey, is an introverted homebody who loves spending extended time by herself, while having a small group of really close friends. But for me as a hyper-extroverted social butterfly who has to work from coffee shops because I just need to be in the *presence* of people, I thrive off having many surface-level relationships to shoot the breeze with, while still maintaining a small group of five people I can regularly connect with at a deeper level. If I were to inhabit Kasey's social life, I would be completely depleted relationally. Hence the subjective nature of loneliness.

But remember, loneliness in itself isn't a bad thing. It's our physiological reminder to have friends. We have to listen to it. However, when left unresolved for extended periods of time, what begins as a helpful motivator can become a chronic illness. And the consequences are devastating.

When we feel lonely for extended periods of time, our bodies enter into a self-preservation mode. This causes our brains to produce extra levels of cortisol, a powerful stress hormone that draws from survival instincts to respond to potential dangers (like encountering a sabertooth tiger during the ice age, or, even worse, taking that advanced chemistry exam). Cortisol doesn't just prepare us to take on physical threats; it also provokes a hyperawareness of potentially dangerous *social* threats and negative social interactions—even if there is no actual threat present in the interaction.[9] That's why we may have a higher sense of distrust toward others if we're chronically lonely, because we've been locked down in self-preservation mode for so long. Further, if any interaction can be perceived as a potential threat, then our chronically lonely selves are less likely to befriend others due to our skepticism and distrust of those who may genuinely want to befriend us. We thus become less enjoyable to be around, causing others to avoid us, which only brings us feelings of shame, disconnection, discouragement, depression, and unworthiness of being loved. These feelings draw us deeper into our loneliness, doubling down on our self-doubt and skepticism of others, catching us in a vicious self-perpetuating vortex of loneliness.[10]

And that's just the beginning.

The elevated level of cortisol and stress that loneliness produces leads to many other health and relational consequences. The neural pathways in our brains begin to suffer upon extended removal from meaningful social interactions, which can yield chronic irritability, anger, depression, addiction, and physical illness.[11] Although the cause-and-effect relationship between loneliness and mental health is blurry (does anxiety and depression cause loneliness, or does loneliness cause anxiety and depression?), what is agreed upon is the two are closely correlated.

Lonely people are more likely to experience mental health issues than those who are not.[12] Counselor and psychologist Mark Mayfield notes that "experiencing mental illness causes us to withdraw from one another, and the loneliness that ensues takes a toll on our mental health. No wonder the rates of depression and anxiety are increasing [in our country]."[13] In fact, psychologist Martin Seligman says, "The rate of depression over the last two generations has increased roughly tenfold."[14] With the mental health crisis also reaching epidemic levels in the United States, especially among teens and young adults, it begs the question: how much does the state of our mental health crisis correlate with the rising rates of loneliness?

Loneliness impacts not only our mental health but our physical health as well. It is one of the main factors associated with a greater risk of coronary heart disease and high blood pressure. There is a correlation between higher amounts of loneliness throughout one's life and greater heart damage. In fact, "lonely heart failure patients were four times as likely as not-lonely heart failure patients to die."[15] It seems we can literally *die* from broken hearts.

Loneliness also contributes to higher risk of stroke and dementia, as well as lower quality sleep.[16] Poor sleep quality impairs our bodies' psychological and physiological repair processes that occur during deep sleep, which results in a more dysfunctional immune system.[17] So, the lonelier we are, the sicker we can get. This is why loneliness and extended social isolation are considered predisease pathways, which are the various biological, psychological, and social factors that can lead to sickness and death. It's been found that loneliness can expedite the onset of other chronic diseases such as cancer, cardiovascular disease, affective disorders, drug or alcohol abuse, chronic obstructive pulmonary disease, sleep disorders, diabetes, and dementia.[18]

Loneliness also increases addictive and impulsive behaviors and impaired judgment.[19] Our brain can actually confuse its need for human connection with other needs. Henry Cloud suggests this happens when we try to connect with "artificial connections"—anything that makes us "feel good"—when we are experiencing the pain of isolation, whether we realize loneliness is the root cause of our pain or not. These artificial connections include any form of addiction, emotional or sexual affairs, job promotions, prestigious awards, major accomplishments, food, sex, pornography, drugs, painkillers, flattery, and so on. Although these things may temporarily alleviate our pain of disconnection, they do not resolve our lack of meaningful connections with others.[20]

All these health consequences are why chronic loneliness increases the odds of early death by 50 *percent*. This makes loneliness more life-threatening than extended exposure to air pollution, obesity, or alcoholism.[21] The impact of loneliness on one's life span is equivalent to the health risk of smoking fifteen cigarettes *a day*.[22] As researcher Susan Mettes notes, "Even when age, sex, chronic diseases, alcohol use, smoking, self-rated health, and physical limitations are accounted for, loneliness still predicts earlier death."[23] Furthermore, studies are finding that deaths of despair, which include suicide and drug overdose, are largely due to increased social isolation and loneliness.[24]

Clearly . . . it is not good to be alone.

ALONE

I think back to that dark spring season of 2020 when I experienced the most crippling depression and anxiety of my life. Obviously, there was a lot going on for everyone. Navigating the uncertainties of a pandemic while being glued to the worldwide infection and death counts on Apple News was reason enough to be anxious and depressed. But there was more at play here in this season of my life.

Just six months prior, Kasey and I had moved away from a city, church, and friend group that we adored. I'd moved to Sioux Falls, South Dakota, in the summer of 2016, after graduating college, to take my first pastoral position and was on staff with the church until September 2019. This church had an incredible culture, both for worship on Sundays and during the workweek. I legitimately went to the office each day feeling like I was working with a family. Some of the best friends I've ever had were on that staff. Additionally, I felt like my work *mattered*. We were all unified around a common purpose to see Jesus set people free through our various ministries. I went to work believing what I did mattered, with people who believed I mattered.

Additionally, Kasey and I had one of the best friend groups we could ever ask for. We were a bunch of young adults navigating the complexities of work, family, and adulthood together, while studying the Word of God on a weekly basis in each other's homes. I had workout buddies, friends I'd run into at my favorite coffee shop, and guy friends with whom I spent hours playing board games. In fact, it was this group of friends who set Kasey and me up on a blind date in July 2018. We were married eight months later.

Needless to say, this was one of the greatest seasons of community I ever had in my life. My intimate, relational, and collective connection needs were all satisfied. But when the phone call came offering me a new position to pursue a dream career in higher education at my alma mater, Indiana Wesleyan University, we jumped on the opportunity. We did what so many of us young adults do: leave our dream community in pursuit of a dream career. In September 2019, we moved away from the city, church, and community we'd come to love so dearly, now in pursuit of this new adventure.

But despite coming back to a place I knew and loved from when I was in college, finding community was way harder than I anticipated. I had a harder time connecting with my coworkers than I did at my previous job, and finding a church that resembled what we had at Ransom Church proved to be even more difficult.

So, in 2020 we were already experiencing relational and collective loneliness pretty seriously to begin with, and then throw a worldwide virus outbreak with stay-at-home orders with no end in sight into the mix? It only exacerbated the feelings of loneliness I already had. That's why it's important to understand that loneliness doesn't just come from extended periods of physical isolation, though it certainly includes those instances. But if anything, loneliness more so stems from not being known—by not having a group of *azarim* (the plural form of *ezer*) just right for you. In his book, *Made for People*, Justin Whitmel Earley describes the subjective nature of loneliness that many of us know all too well:

> What I mean by loneliness is this: the feeling of being a person who used to have friends. . . . Many of us have experienced being an outcast, but that's only one version of loneliness. There are many, and they do not all look the same. . . . Loneliness comes from losing a loved one. Loneliness comes from moving away. It comes from changing churches or seeing a small group dissolve. Loneliness comes from being excluded or breaking up. It comes from divorce or being hurt by someone. But often, strangely, it

also comes when you're surrounded by everyone but don't feel known by anyone. Loneliness is the ache for something you used to have. Often an ache you cannot even name. As if relationship drifted away silently during the night, and you woke up in a world you cannot explain.[25]

The interviewees in my research recalled similar feelings. Zach belonged to a friend group of "nerd friends" and another friend group of "Christian friends," each representative of important aspects of his life. However, he didn't feel fully understood by either group, because each group didn't seem to understand the interests of the opposite quality in his personality. "It's hard to find that kind of 'nerd-dom' that welcomes Christians," Zach said. "And it's hard to find super nerdy board game groups within Christian communities as well. So wherever I go, there's a part of me that's lonely."

Or take Shae, who recalled experiencing loneliness particularly during her freshman and sophomore years of college. Shae's friends at the time didn't understand how her newfound faith in Jesus animated her sense of purpose and meaning, and because of that, she found these other friendships more surface level and less satisfying. As she reflected,

> There were still times that I felt lonely in a whole different aspect because nobody understood the deeper meaning that I was searching for and trying to embed myself in, because I lost all of the friends that I had at the first stage of my college life—the friends that were surface level. I didn't even have those really at all anymore, because we had even less in common than we already did. So, I remember feeling lonely because nobody really *understood*. (emphasis added)

Stewart and Justin both experienced loneliness when they moved to start a new season of life in Vermillion, South Dakota, the college town in which I pastor. Justin particularly reflected on the adjustment to working an "adult" nine-to-five job in a small empty office with minimal connection to his coworkers. He admitted taking for granted the consistency of being surrounded by friends while at college, realizing now that a larger effort is required to coordinate get-togethers with high school and college friends while being a working adult. Justin said he was surprised by "how hard it can be to reach out even when people are close."

Another self-reported cause for loneliness was being in crowds or groups with whom the interviewees lacked connection. Zach said he felt the loneliest when he was in a crowd of people just going their own way. James, an introvert who embraces a life of solitude, said, "Situation wise, it doesn't really matter if I'm around a lot of people or if I'm by myself, because sometimes I feel less lonely by myself than I do with certain types of people." Briana made an important distinction between being alone and being lonely when she said, "I love being alone, but I don't love being lonely. . . . I can be in a room full of people and be completely lonely and feel completely alone, even though I'm in fact not alone."

All that to say, the causes for loneliness are all across the board due to their highly subjective nature. But despite the different causes, loneliness produced a variety of negative thoughts and feelings in my interviewees, such as sad, empty, defeated, lost, disconnected, misunderstood, shut down, anxious, having a lack of purpose, and tearful. Thoughts that accompanied these feelings were, "These friendships will never last," "Is this what my career will be like?" "My relationships peaked in college," and "What's the point?"

———

Clearly, it is not good to be alone. God himself said it, and the science backs it up. Although loneliness serves as that "check engine" light for our need for human connection, when left unchecked for too long, it can wreak havoc on our minds, bodies, and souls.

Thankfully, God is the ultimate problem solver, and when he finally gave Adam his ezer, he remedied his loneliness for good.

DISCUSSION QUESTIONS

1. Discuss a time when you felt lonely. What were some of the reasons or causes for your loneliness?
2. What do you think about the idea of loneliness being a "check engine" light for your need to connect with others? Does that change your perception of loneliness at all?
3. What most surprised you about the effects loneliness has on our minds, bodies, and souls?
4. Loneliness doesn't just occur during instances of physical isolation but when feeling misunderstood by others. Do you find this to be true? Why or why not?

CHAPTER 2

DESIGNED FOR COMMUNITY

At last! . . . This one is bone from my bone,
and flesh from my flesh.

– Genesis 2:23 –

"Bartle doo."

. . .

"Bartle doo..."

. . .

"Bartle doo? Bartle dee?"

. . .

"Bartle doo tacos with the ting tal and the cow happies with the blartum burgers? "

. . .

"I *said*, bartle doo *tacos* with the *ting tal* and the *cow happies* with the *blartum burgers*. . . ? Cramp mul stank, man."

. . .

Confused? I was, too, when I started hanging out with Tyler, Nathan, and Brice.

Freshman year of high school marked the beginning of a new era. Not just because I was (finally) wrapping up my journey through puberty, or because I got a new locker in the senior high wing of my school. It was because I made new friends.

Tyler and Nathan were new students at Northeastern High School that same year, and they were already good friends with Brice, a junior at NHS. We'd rubbed shoulders for the first time the previous summer during our competitive marching band season, and before we knew it, I'd kindled a friendship with these three guys.

But the more I started hanging out with Tyler, Nathan, and Brice, the more I noticed they kept saying "bartle doo" for *everything* (or, to quote it in full, bartle doo tacos with the ting tal and the cow happies with the blartum burgers). They claimed it was a phrase you could use to mean anything you want, but it was most often used as a greeting or salutation. "Bartle doo, Nathan! How are you?" "Oh, I'm bartle doin', Tyler. How about yourself?"

Yeah, I know. I thought they were crazy too.

As it turns out, "bartle doo" was a phrase they picked up from a late 2000s YouTuber named EdBassMaster (this was way before being a professional YouTuber was mainstream). And yet, despite how ridiculous this stupid phrase was, I noticed that the more I hung out with them, the more I started saying "bartle do." All. The. Time. "Bartle do" became such a core part of my vernacular that the phrase followed me through the remainder of high school and even on to *college*.

What my adoption of this ridiculous phrase has taught me is that the people with whom we surround ourselves influence who we are, what we say, what we do, and what we value. This includes how you like your steak cooked because your dad taught you the proper way to eat a steak, the way you manage money because of the way your family of origin handled finances, the inside jokes you tell among your friends, how you enunciate certain words because of whom you talk with most of the day, and even how you conduct your life due to of your nation's culture.

Put simply, you are who you're with. That's because God designed you for community.

REMEDYING LONELINESS

We left off in Genesis 2 when God saw it was not good for Adam to be alone. He gave Adam the job of naming all the animals, in the hope one of them would be the perfect ezer for him—a helper on whom he could depend. "But still there was no helper just right for him," as verse 20 says.

God gets to the bottom of it. Genesis 2:21–24 reads,

> So the LORD God caused the man to fall into a deep sleep. While the man slept, the LORD God took out one of the man's ribs and closed up the opening. Then the LORD God made a woman from the rib, and he brought her to the man.
>
> > "At last!" the man exclaimed.
> > "This one is bone from my bone,
> >   and flesh from my flesh!
> > She will be called 'woman,'
> >   because she was taken from 'man.'"
>
> This explains why a man leaves his father and mother and is joined to his wife, and the two are united into one.

"At last!" Adam cried. You can almost hear a sigh of relief beneath Adam's words. "At last, I am *not alone*," Adam seems to say. What we see in Genesis 2 isn't just the union of man and woman in the first marriage. We also see the first human friendship. The creation account not only sets the precedent for the union between God and humankind, and for marriage between a man and a woman, but also for the necessity for friendship.

Again, despite its lack of goodness, Adam's loneliness existed before the fall precisely because Adam was made perfect, albeit incomplete. God worked diligently to find Adam a "suitable helper" because he was finishing the task of designing humanity to reflect his own image. We are distinguished from the rest of creation precisely because God says, "Let us make mankind in our *image*, in our *likeness*" (Genesis 1:26 NIV, emphasis added). The word *image* found in this verse implies a "mirror-like representation." The image of God, then, ultimately serves as the model for how we ought to act and live in accordance to God's intentions and design at creation.[26] So if we want to understand our highly relational nature, first we need to look deeply within the image of God.

There are several aspects to God's image that we as humans are called to carry out according to his design. The seventeenth-century revivalist and theologian John Wesley categorized the image of God into three dimensions: the political image, the moral image, and the natural image.

The political image represents God's command for us to "govern" the earth and "reign" over it (Genesis 1:28). Since we are the pinnacle of creation, God calls us to be cocreators and co-laborers with him to steward the earth, care for creation, and do good and meaningful work through our vocations. That's why we love working on projects, striving toward goals, and making the world a better place.

Second, the moral image represents God's command for us "to be perfect, even as your Father in heaven is perfect" (Matthew 5:48). God is a perfectly moral and righteous God, and he created us with the same capacity to exercise love, goodness, kindness, justice, righteousness, and all other virtues that make up God's holy character. Unfortunately, because the power of sin is still at work, we won't fully recover the moral image of God until Jesus returns to make all things new.

That then leaves the natural image of God. The natural image primarily includes our ability to exercise free will to live according to God's character and design for our lives. If the moral image defines the moral standard we are meant to live, then the natural image is our ability to live out those standards he instills in us or not. For example, since God is love, we also can choose to love or not. Or since God exercises logic and reason, we also can choose to exercise logic and reason. Therefore, a key truth we can learn about ourselves from the natural image of God is this: we are designed to live in community because *God* lives in community.

When you read Genesis 1:26, notice how God says, "Let *us* make human beings in *our* image" (emphasis added).

This is probably one of the most significant uses of the plural form of the first-person possessive pronoun you'll ever read, because it attests to the communal nature of the Trinity. One of the core doctrines of the Christian faith is that we believe in one God in *three persons*: the Father, the Son, and the Holy Spirit. What's funny about this major tenet of our faith, though, is the word *trinity* doesn't show up in Scripture at all. However, the reality of the Trinity is most certainly implied. Jesus himself would reference how he is the Son of God and lives in perfect relationship with God the Father, and that the Son and the Father would send the Holy Spirit to live among us.

The New Testament is riddled with references to one God being three persons. The only problem was there wasn't any formal language to communicate this phenomenon adequately. So all the early church leaders came together at a big meeting, called the Council of Nicaea (pronounced nie-SEE-uh) in 325 AD, to figure this out. How could God be both *one* God and *three*? As they discussed, they came to the conclusion that the Greek word best able to communicate this was *prosopon*. In English, it's translated as "person."[27]

To us, the word *person* is used interchangeably with the word *individual*. But that could not be further from the early church fathers' intent with the word. As it relates to the Trinity, the word *person* communicates one who is in relationship with others. We cannot understand who the person of the Father is without understanding how he relates to the Son and the Holy Spirit. We cannot understand who the Son is without understanding how he relates to the Holy Spirit and the Father. And we cannot understand who the Holy Spirit is without understanding how he relates to the Father and the Son. The Trinity is one God in three persons who *perfectly* rely on each other and serve one another in holy love. That's why when we say we worship "one" God, his oneness is in reference to his perfect, indivisible, inseparable community of love between the three divine persons.

Therefore, when God says, "Let *us* make human beings in *our* image," he is referring to his own communal nature as one God in three persons. For us as humans to bear the full natural image of the Triune God, then, means we also must live as *persons* who operate in webs of selflessly loving relationships and community ourselves.[28] This is why Adam's ability to bear the image of God was not fully possible *until* God created Eve. This wasn't true because of a marital or sexual union between them, since unmarried persons still powerfully reflect the image of God, but because of the chance for Adam to find—in Eve—a fellow image-bearer with whom he could commune and depend upon.

The declaration that humanity was "very good" in Genesis chapter 1 is the culmination of God addressing the one thing that was "not good" in chapter 2: loneliness.[29]

We are relational because God himself is relational. The communion of the three divine persons is so vital to who God is that he designed humanity to reflect that same communal nature. Adam's isolation is as contradictory to human nature as one of the divine persons being separate from the other two. From the very beginning, humankind was designed to exist in community, both with God and with each other.

And that's not just what Scripture says. It's what science says as well. While the consequences of loneliness are devastating, what is equally startling are the benefits of living in community.

HARDWIRED FOR CONNECTION

We are a gregarious species hardwired for connection with others.[30] Jonathan Haidt, a moral psychologist, says, "We are an ultra-social species, full of emotions finely tuned for loving, befriending, helping, sharing, and otherwise intertwining our lives with others."[31] Haidt goes on to say that "having strong social relationships strengthens the immune system, extends life expectancy (more than does quitting smoking), speeds recovery from surgery, and reduces the risks of depression and anxiety disorders."[32] Susan Pinker notes that "playing cards once a week or meeting friends every Wednesday night at Starbucks adds as many years to our lives as taking beta blockers or quitting a pack-a-day habit."[33] Robin Dunbar, another psychology researcher, also writes about how we are less likely to get diseases and have longer life expectancy the more friends we have.[34] You would think that the cause of long-term survival rates would be due to things like eating a healthy diet, avoiding excessive alcohol consumption, maintaining good physical fitness, or even avoiding exposure to air pollution. But studies show that the best predictors of long-term survival rates come down to having a high sense of social support and belonging to a social network. In fact, having a strong group of friends and community to belong to can increase survival rates by as much as 50 percent.[35] This is most likely because regularly enjoying time with meaningful friends produces more endorphins than if you were living a more isolated life. Dunbar says,

> Endorphins stimulate the release of the body's natural killer cells, one of the white blood cells that act as the immune system's shock troops in searching out and destroying the bacteria and viruses that make us sick. It seems that the endorphins triggered by the presence of friends tune the immune system and give us enhanced resistance to the bugs that are responsible for many of the diseases that so discomfort us.[36]

So it appears that laughter is truly some of the best medicine.

Friendships can also have this extensive impact on our minds and bodies because quality connections with others release another powerful chemical in our brains, called oxytocin—the master chemical of social connection (or sometimes referred to as "the cuddle hormone"). This is the same chemical that gets released when a mom gives birth to a baby. Her mind gets flooded with oxytocin to strengthen the initial bonding process with her newborn. Similarly, when we receive an act of charity, such as a hug, smile, or word of encouragement, our brains release oxytocin to generate the feelings associated with being loved, valued, and cherished. Oxytocin keeps us calm, regulates social interactions, reinforces group cohesion, releases stress, increases pain tolerance, and reduces distractibil-ity (all the while making childbearing just a little more tolerable).[37] The effects of oxytocin are literally the complete opposite of what cortisol, our stress hormone, does when we undergo long periods of isolation and loneliness.

So oxytocin is what binds us closer together, making us feel more loved and cherished, which conversely releases more endorphins, granting us a better immune system, a healthier body, and a longer life. Truly, "faithful friends are life-saving medicine."[38]

But that's not all. Beyond the physiological benefits of human relationship, people who are connected in significant social net-works have a greater sense of meaning and purpose in their lives.[39]

The quality of our life is largely influenced by the quality of our community. Henry Cloud says our most significant relation-ships can determine

- How long we live
- Whether we reach our goals or not
- How much money we make
- How well our kids do in school
- How much we trust others
- How we cope with stress and failure
- What kind of mood we are in
- How much physical pain we experience
- How and what we think[40]

Remember: you are who you're with.

If I'm surrounded with friends who say "bartle doo tacos" all the time, I'm also going to say "bartle doo tacos" all the time. But that doesn't just apply to our catch phrases and sense of humor. It applies to our eating habits, work ethics, values, physical health, emotional management, outlook on life, and so much more. For example, some studies have shown that couples on the brink of divorce happen to spend time with others whose marriages are also falling apart, and those who have healthy marriages happen to befriend couples in healthy marriages. Similarly, people with active lifestyles are friends with others who enjoy physical fitness and healthy living, or people are more likely to quit smoking if they have friends who are actively trying to quit smoking as well.[41]

Again, you are who you're with.

This is all due in large part to the neuroplasticity of our brains. They are always changing, adapting, and growing based on our experiences and surrounding environments, which especially include our interpersonal relationships as a major contributing factor.[42] The quality and depth of our relationships really do impact what we do and who we become. Amy Banks, a specialist in relational psychopharmacology who helps those suffering from chronic disconnection, asserts that "the chemistry of healthy relationships enhances your ability to change your old patterns."[43] In other words, if you want to change any part of your life, whether that's a gambling habit, a negative thought life, or your eating patterns, you need to surround ourselves with people who can reinforce the identity, habits, and lifestyle you want to adapt. However, the opposite can also be the case as well. If you are consistently involved in damaging relationships or dangerous environments, your brain will create neural pathways and habits that adapt to those environments and reinforce self-destructive behavior.

Another factor regarding the formational power of your friendships is the consistency of friends in your life. The people you spend the most time with, whether by sharing your physical presence or occupying your mental space, are the relationships that shape your brain the most, no matter how good, bad, or strained they are.

Banks says, "The more time you spend in a relationship, regardless of whether it is mutual or abusive, the more that relationship is actively shaping your central nervous system."[44]

At the risk of being redundant, I'll say it one more time: you are who you're with.

The quality of our closest relationships is a heavily weighted determining factor in who we become. That's why having good, significant community with others can enhance the overall quality of our life. Haidt comments again, "We are ultra-social creatures, and we can't be happy without having friends and secure attachments to other people."[45] Vivek Murthy, who served as the US Surgeon General, notes,

> We all have a deep and abiding need to be seen for who we are— as fully dimensional, complex, and vulnerable human beings. We all need to know that we matter and that we are loved. These are the deep-seated needs that secure relationships satisfy, and when they are met, we tend to live healthier, more productive, and more rewarding lives. When they go unmet, we suffer.[46]

To bring it all home, John Cacioppo, our leading scientist on loneliness, says,

> Our brains and bodies are designed to function in aggregates, not in isolation. That is the essence of an obligatory gregarious species. The attempt to function in denial of our need for others, whether that need is great or small in any given individual, violates our design specifications. The effects on health are warning signs, similar to the "Check Engine" light that comes on in today's cars with their computerized senses. But social connection is not just a lubricant that, like motor oil, prevents overheating and wear. Social connection is a fundamental part of the human operating (and organizing) system itself.[47]

———

It's not good to be alone because we are designed for community.

You need friends. I need friends. We all *need* friends to be the best versions of ourselves. That's how God originally intended it.

And yet . . .

Despite the sheer amount of evidence that we are at our best when we are in significant community with others, it's staggering to think the three in five Americans who sometimes or always feel alone don't fully experience these benefits, that four in five young adults between the ages of eighteen and twenty-four don't live into their God-given design for community, and how people of color and those from lower socioeconomic statuses experience disproportionately higher rates of loneliness in comparison to middle- and upper-class white people. The thought of such a large amount of people in our population suffering from the consequences of prolonged loneliness is truly alarming.

If we are far better off living in community, why are we so lonely? How did we get here? How do we, in the United States of America, have such high rates of loneliness, despite having everything else going for us as far as freedoms and economic opportunities are concerned?

Why is our need for friends at an all-time high?

Well, as it turns out, we've done this to ourselves. A central truth to the human experience is that we are products of our environment. As we just learned, who we are, what we do, and what we value are influenced by the people we're with. This happens on a micro level, like the inside jokes you start saying because of your friend group, or the Christmas traditions you practice because of what you've always done with your family. But it also happens at a macro level, like embracing a lifestyle according to the values upheld by a state or a nation. That is what a nation is, after all—a giant collection of people who influence each other.

Our cultures form us, and they often do so through means that are unseen and subconscious. That's why sometimes the only way you can discover your environmental influences is by stepping outside that environment and realizing there is a whole other way of life outside the one you've grown so accustomed to (for example, how crazy you sound when you say "bartle doo" to a group of strangers). You may realize in those instances how good you've got it when compared to other people. But you may also realize how much better things could be if you change how you operate.

That's the case with our culture.

Something is fueling the loneliness epidemic. Unlike disease epidemics, where some mutated strain can get released into the air that infects you when you come into contact with it against your will, cultural epidemics are created by ourselves intentionally, though often subconsciously. Loneliness at epidemic proportions does not just "happen." You can't just get infected by a loneliness outbreak like the common cold. Your immune system is designed to heal itself, learn the new mutation of the common cold, and help you feel better. But your body doesn't automatically heal your loneliness. We might certainly find ourselves lonelier in certain seasons and scenarios than other periods or spaces in our life, but I argue that the ongoing, prolonged, chronic state of loneliness we're seeing in our nation is because of various cultural values and lifestyles that we choose to embrace. Paul tells us not to "conform to the pattern of this world" because we are easily formed by our world (Romans 12:2 NIV). It takes a lot of effort and intentionality to fight against the cultural forces that form us, and if we're not careful, we can all become products of our lonely environment.

There are so many theories and possibilities for what exactly is fueling the loneliness epidemic in our world right now, especially in regard to the disproportionately high rates among Gen Zers, that go far beyond the scope of this book. But in the next two chapters, I want to address at least two possible cultural drivers that are influencing us to lead lonelier lives, especially regarding young adults. The first is individualism, which declares the cultural mantra of "I don't need anyone else." The second is isolationism, which declares the cultural mantra of "I don't want anyone else."

DISCUSSION QUESTIONS

1. What's something you do, say, or value that you can specifically attribute to someone else's influence on your life?
2. What do you think about God existing as a community of three divine persons? Why is this important to understand when we consider our own relational nature?
3. What benefits of friendship surprised you the most?
4. Can you think of a time when you were at your happiest and healthiest that you could attribute back to the friends you had in your life?

CHAPTER 3

"I DON'T NEED ANYONE ELSE"

No one should seek their own good,
but the good of others.

– 1 Corinthians 10:24 (NIV) –

I was shocked by how at-home I felt when I visited another country.

I went on a missions trip to Zambia with the church I had just come on staff with in 2016. The goal of this trip was to partner with the Zambians who were already doing ministry in their community. We were just there for the ride. And it was absolutely incredible. Sure, we got to see some amazing things while we were there, like Victoria Falls, one of the seven natural wonders of the world; the sunset over the Zambezi River with the mist from the falls off in the distance; the lions, elephants, giraffes, and rhinos on the game drive we took in the country. As cool as all those experiences were, what blew me away the most were the people.

Zambia embraces an entirely different way of life than I was used to. When I was there, things moved at a much slower pace. It wasn't the clock that determined when events started and stopped; it was whenever everyone decided to arrive. Church would last for about three hours, and it would end whenever they decided to be done, because they enjoyed basking in the presence of God with each other that much. They didn't have lunch plans to get to or afternoon football games they had to watch. Life moved at such a different pace than I had ever experienced in the States.

The primary reason for this major cultural difference was because *relationships* drove everything they did.

Plumbers wouldn't start a repair job on a leaky faucet until he could honor the head of the household first. They waited until everyone arrived at church because they didn't want to start worship without anyone missing out. Even how they went about managing their possessions was driven by their commitment to relationship. I remember two of the Zambians we were ministering with were playing around with each other by stealing a hat back and forth. When Marpeh got a hold of the hat, she sarcastically said, "Oh look, I'm *sooo* Western. This is *my* hat. M*yyyyy* hat." And as I looked at her in confusion, she went on to say, "In Zambia, you don't say it's *my* hat, because it's *our* hat."

Perhaps I felt so at home because I felt like I belonged to a family. Their relational connectedness was so strong that it was embedded into the very fabric of their society at a level that far exceeds that of the United States. Even the people we worked with in poverty were some of the happiest people I had ever met, because they had God and each other. That's not to diminish the severity of their living experiences at all, but their happiness despite their poverty was so brazenly counterintuitive to what I had expected. If they had each other, it seemed they had their needs met.

This is the polar opposite of what we experience in our country because Zambia, like most of the world throughout human history, is a collectivist culture that radically values relationships, whereas the United States is an individualist culture that radically values the individual.[48] And this may have a significant role to play in our loneliness epidemic.

COLLECTIVIST CULTURES VERSUS INDIVIDUALIST CULTURES

Collectivists, like my friends in Zambia, live according to a "group comes first" mentality that heavily emphasizes relationships and social networks.[49] Every individual is connected to a greater web of relationships with a social obligation to honor, respect, and commit to everyone found within that hierarchy of relationships.[50] This is why service providers, like the plumber I mentioned, do not start on a job until they can honor the head person in that social context.

Collectivists' highly relational nature is due to how they define the self. Their individual sense of self is ultimately driven by how connected he or she is to their greater social context, like a family, church, or community. Therefore, a collectivist will adjust his or her personal desires and actions for whatever benefits the whole group.[51] Hence, if someone knows another person needs a hat on a particularly sunny day, he will give up his hat if he doesn't need it, because it is truly *their* hat after all. Or instead of starting an event at a certain time so everyone can get to their next thing afterward that ultimately serves themselves, they delay starting so that *everyone* can benefit *equally* from not having missed anything. Living with a "group comes first" mentality makes a world of difference.

If you think that isn't radical enough, consider how collectivists go about pursuing their careers. People in collectivist societies usually don't decide to leave their families to pursue their "dream job" as a botanist in Portland 1,200 miles away from home. Rather, it's common practice for people to stay local and continue working in the family business or trade. Why? Because providing for the greater social context, which is normally their families, is more important to them than pursuing their individual dreams. This "group comes first" mentality even affects how they go about marriage. Collectivists' marriages aren't so much about the individual sense of romance between the couple who hit it off at the local bar-and-grill's trivia night and decide to enter into a relationship. Rather, collectivists' *families* arrange their marriages—and the couple enters into it *willingly*. This is because the arranged marriage brings the two families together in a new alliance that strengthens them both. The collectivist couple, then, is even willing to leverage their *romantic interests* to better serve their group.

Collectivist cultures were, and continue to be, the dominant way humans operate in the world. But collectivism sounds so radical to us because we in the United States live in a "radically individualist" culture.[52] Unlike collectivists, individualists define the self by *separating* from the social context to express and expand upon our personal uniqueness. Instead of a "group comes first" mentality, we value self-reliance, independence, and personal freedom to choose whatever is best for us, sometimes even at the expense of others. We cringe at the thought of being "obligated" to anything because it eliminates the possibility of exercising our personal freedom to do whatever we want (like delaying RSVPing for your second cousin's high school graduation party because you're waiting for a better offer; we've all done it). As individualists, it's rare to adjust our desires and actions for whatever benefits the group, because we would rather pursue what benefits ourselves individually. That doesn't mean we never help our friends or serve others during times of need, but it's not nearly as intuitive nor to the extent as those in collectivist cultures.

Now, let me be clear. There are many elements about our individualist culture that I love. One of the critiques of collectivist cultures is that it can be easy for us to lose our sense of self and autonomy because *everything* revolves around serving others. The United States is supposed to be the land of opportunity. We are given the freedom to become whoever we want to become. We can pull ourselves up by our bootstraps to get it done because there isn't anyone holding us back. The empowerment that comes to us as individuals from this value is significant and shouldn't be downplayed.

However, when taken too far, individualism makes life entirely about *ourselves* instead of about living with others as we're designed to do. Now it's all about *you*. It's about what *you* do, what *you* get, what *you* wear, what *you* eat, how *you* express *yourself*, who *you* date, where *you* work, how *you* define *your* destiny. Even our relationships become more focused on forming our individual uniqueness or meeting our preferences or making us feel good. If life as individualists is all about furthering ourselves, then it becomes one brutal competition of one-upping others around us or always being beaten out by somebody else. Author and theologian Andy Root says,

> Individualism, in the end, kills relationship because it does not see the human being as bound to others in mutuality and love. Individualism sees all your interactions as the playing field of some competitive game. Others become objects because I only know and engage them as functions. My coworker and a broom

are essentially the same; they both support or assist me in get-ting what I want.[53]

In other words, we opt to keep our hats for ourselves.

YOU-DO-YOU-ISM AND ELECTIVE IDENTITIES

If left unchecked, it's only a matter of time before our radical indi-vidualism leads us to a more isolated lifestyle where the "self" reigns supreme. This is the unique form of individualism that Gen Z embraces. David Brooks noted that previous US generations valued "economic individualism," where everyone was free to pull them-selves up by their bootstraps to build their homes, families, careers, and financial prosperity. But younger generations are now embrac-ing a "lifestyle individualism," where you are free to be whoever you want to be. It's not so much about financial prosperity and building the life you want external to yourself, but rather about who you are *internally* and the unique way you express yourself. And perhaps there is no greater phrase that sums up this new form of individu-alism than what I call "you-do-you-ism."

"You do you" is the phrase of tolerance. It's what you say when you don't necessarily agree with how someone conducts their life, but you say anyway, "Who am I to judge? You are your own person. *You do you*." You-do-you-ism is the freedom to be whoever you want to be with no consequences, all while respecting everyone else's personal (read, *individualized*) choices. David Kinnaman and Mark Matlock describe this trend among Gen Zers as someone's "elective identity," which "is the idea that people can and should define their own identity, [because] the individual . . . is the ultimate arbiter of what is true about herself or himself."[54] According to the Gen Z per-spective, identity springs forth from looking inside oneself, pursuing one's desires, listening to one's own feelings above all else, and doing whatever he or she wants as long as it does not hurt anyone else. When a life is centered on ego, one's identity hinges on the ability to achieve whatever is desired.

And you might be thinking, *What's so wrong with that? Is it that big of a deal to have complete freedom over how I see myself? And how does it affect our loneliness?* The problem arises when we try to form our identities solely based on how we feel and what we want to hear without the wise support of others in a community to whom we can submit, honor, and listen.

Elective identity and you-do-you-ism is at the core of our post-modern, post-Christian, radically individualist Western society. Taken to its furthest extreme, I'm not only free to define my unique identity, but I am also free to define my own *morality*. Whatever is true and good is what ultimately serves *me*, and what is best for me might not be best for others, but my expectation is for them to respect it anyway. Further, if they call me out for it—even if it is damaging to myself in the long run—then they're intolerant and judgmental. Therefore, since there is no sense of truly knowing what is right and wrong, everyone should just respect each other's differing sense of morality. Even if someone doesn't agree with how I conduct myself, instead of discussing it, they simply tolerate it as long as my behavior does not hurt anybody else or infringe on another's ability to exercise their own personal freedoms.[55] "You do you."

So how does this all relate to loneliness?

If the self is the arbiter of everything we do, then friendships ultimately become self-seeking. They are not necessarily based on the mutual self-giving nature of good, deep friendships that challenge us in our shortcomings and pull us out of our potentially wrongful and even harmful internal desires. Rather, according to this viewpoint, friendships are all about satisfying our elected identities and justifying our elastic morality. The pursuit of authentic community with others who know us fully and invite us into a better life *outside* our internal sense of self gets distorted into tribalism, which is the phenomenon of belonging to groups who affirm our identity statements and agree on our selected truth. When conforming to tribalism, we tend to be very defensive against anyone outside our "tribe." However, the irony about tribalistic groups is they don't necessarily care about our soul or challenge us. In fact, we may tend to *further* lose our sense of self in these tribalistic groups, becoming someone we never intended to begin with, all because it's more about belonging to a tribe that enforces a certain persona than it is to be fully known for who we are without the fear of them leaving us.

Friends are supposed to push us and stretch us. They aren't meant to be people who unanimously agree with us, affirm everything we do, and make us feel good no matter what. Through this radically individualist viewpoint, friends are more like products we consume to serve our individualistic sense of self.

FRIENDS AS PRODUCTS TO CONSUME

I am an Apple sheep. That's the official term that someone on the internet deemed for the crazed individuals who worship Apple products with a cultish following. I have been a Mac user ever since I was in sixth grade. The only mobile phone I have ever owned is an iPhone. My most visited website is MacRumors.com, a news site solely dedicated to all the potential rumors surrounding Apple products and the tech landscape. I watch every Apple keynote highlighting its latest software updates and product releases, and then watch countless hours of techy YouTubers reviewing the announcements and products.

Yes, I know. I have a problem.

One of the things Apple does so well (especially to its religious followers like myself) is its marketing. Every time a new product is released, I am sucked into its messaging wondering how I could justify the purchase of an Apple Vision Pro headset to make my life better somehow (*cough* I can't! *cough*). But alas, through my obsession with Apple products, I have fallen into the grasp of American consumerism: that constant desire to get more stuff in the hope that it will make my life better and happier.

Our consumerism is another driving factor in our radically individualist culture. The value of consumerism began with the economic boom following World War II.[56] People worked extreme hours and earned lots of money to chase away the sting of scarcity and consume products that met personal desires and expressed individuality. Now, consumption in itself isn't bad. All of us need to consume stuff in order to live. The problem is when it becomes a constant pursuit of satisfying our unnecessary wants to unhealthy levels, hungering for more and more. Companies' marketing departments are a masterclass in convincing us that we need something when, in fact, we don't.

However, a consequential characteristic of consumerism is if the product doesn't satisfy our expectations, then it can always be returned. The mentality of living in a consumerism-driven culture, as author Skye Jethani puts it, is to assume that "the world will accommodate to your desires" and "you shouldn't settle for anything less than the fulfillment of your precise expectations."[57] If it *doesn't* meet your expectations, then you can return it and proceed to give it a seething one-star review on Amazon, expressing your sour disappointment and ~~un~~justified rage.

The reason we need to grapple with our consumeristic tendencies is because they inevitably pervert our approach to relationships.

Under the influence of consumerism, people can become "products" used to benefit ourselves. They become fun, pleasurable means that make us feel better. We play video games with them, go out to the bar, study with them, go horseback riding, and take lunch breaks with them. And all of these are great activities to do with our friends—again, friends are *meant* to make life better. But what we need to be aware of is if any of our motivations behind cultivating our friendships are strictly self-seeking instead of mutually self-sacrificing; if so, we may be approaching our friendships with a consumeristic mind-set. When an individualistic worldview expects that *all* of life—including our relationships—should meet our precise expectations, then we can abandon a friendship as soon as it gets too difficult and is no longer self-serving. One star. Two thumbs down. Do not recommend.

Under consumerism, friendships are less akin to covenants based on selfless love and more like contracts that fulfill personal needs.[58] Commitment and obligation leave a bitter taste in the mouth of individualism. Jethani describes consumerism's influence on relationships this way: "[People] make calculated decisions about which community will offer the most comfortable environment, and [their] commitment to that group lasts only as long as the comfort endures. . . . It's the tension between choice and commitment, between comfort and community."[59]

Of course, there are instances where friendships become toxic and are no longer beneficial to our well-being. Friendships of this sort should be ended after attempts at reconciliation have been exhausted. But aside from those cases, this is why people insist on tribalism over community: tribe mates are meant to keep us comfortable and function within the expectations we place upon them to reinforce who we are, what we do, and what we value. Anyone who challenges that is either asked to leave, or we leave ourselves. In his book *The Connected Life*, Dr. Todd Hall sums this all up perfectly when he writes,

> There are many interrelated factors that led to our current connection crisis. In some ways they can all be tied back to cultural trends that steadily grew in the last half of the twentieth century—the collective consciousness of the American mind about what constitutes the 'good life'—what we might call 'the American ideal.' This set of ideologies, values, and beliefs that constitute the American ideal include extreme forms of individualism and materialism. This 'good life' values independence over friendship, personal comfort over commitment to others, solitary achievements over the common good, and economic success over social and emotional well-being.[60]

"I DON'T NEED ANYONE ELSE . . ." BUT YOU DO

Those of us who are products of our radically individualist culture embrace its mantra that "I don't need anyone else." We want to connect with friends to make us feel good, but disconnect from friends when we feel bad. Doing all the fun things together is great. But connecting on a deeper level to reveal our deepest weaknesses? Nuh uh. No way. We enjoy having friends because they make us feel good and affirm our elected identities and elastic morality—but do we *need* them? That would be considered weak, wouldn't it? Codependent even. Thus, we insist that friendships need to be strictly fun and pleasurable, not supportive. Suppress your weaknesses at all costs. You don't need anyone to help you, anyway. Just do it yourself. And don't get too close. Don't let them know who you truly are. Don't let them in on how you truly feel—that your life is completely falling apart.

"I. Don't. Need. Them."

But you do.

"I. Can. Do. This. All. By. My. Self."

But you can't.

We fake ourselves out when we declare that we "don't need anyone else." In all seriousness, we *need* friends. No matter how independent we think we are, we're wrong. Brené Brown says, "As members of a social species, we don't derive strength from our rugged individualism, but rather from our collective ability to plan, communicate, and work together. Our neural, hormonal, and genetic makeup support interdependence over independence."[61]

God designed you to rely on him and others. We are better together. I don't think it's a coincidence that the fall of Adam and Eve occurred when the serpent lured them to disobey God with the same temptation individualism offers us: that we can become our own god and take matters into our hands. That's the essence of sin, is it not? After Eve tried to hold her ground with God's command not to eat from the forbidden tree, the serpent proved all the more cunning:

> "You won't die!" the serpent replied to the woman. "God knows that your eyes will be opened as soon as you eat it, and you will be like God, knowing both good and evil."
>
> The woman was convinced. She saw that the tree was beautiful and its fruit looked delicious, and she wanted the wisdom it would give her. So she took some of the fruit and ate it. Then she gave some to her husband, who was with her, and he ate it, too. (Genesis 3:4–6)

Am I saying individualism comes from the devil? No. But when we stray away from God by becoming our own gods, worshipping ourselves to define what's right and wrong for selfish gain, all while utilizing relationships to accomplish our personalized desires, then we are missing the mark of how God wants us to live—in interdependent union with him *and* others. Sin separates us, and it will take advantage of our radically individualist culture to keep us separated and alone, ever convincing us that we are our own self-sufficient gods.

Here's what's fascinating, though. A study published in July 2024 called the American Friendship Project sought to be "the most accurate and most complete account of American friendship" due to a lack of comprehensive studies on the nature of friendships in our nation.[62] What it found was despite all the reports about our loneliness epidemic, Americans have more friends than previously thought. The results reported that 55–60 percent of the sample indicated having "close" or "best" friends, with an additional 23 percent indicating having "just" casual friends. Only 3 percent of the study's sample reported having no friends at all. Overall, 75 percent were satisfied with how many friends they had, and 66 percent were satisfied with how they maintained their friendships.

This is all great news! But a key question is how do we reconcile these statistics of Americans' satisfaction with their friendships and the reports of increased rates of loneliness? My theory is it all lies within the lack of intimacy, dependence, and closeness with our friends. In light of American's satisfaction with their friendships, the American Friendship Project also reported the following:

> There was also a clear sense that Americans longed for greater closeness with their friends. Over 40 percent felt they were not as close to their friends as they would like, and less than half felt that they were satisfied with the amount of time they had with friends. Surprisingly, this was true for college students and adults alike. . . . Nearly half agreed that it is difficult to make friends.[63]

This could line up with the stats I shared in the introduction that two in five Americans (43 percent) sometimes or always feel that their relationships are not meaningful, one in four Americans (27 percent) rarely or never feel as though there are people who really understand them, and one in five people report they rarely or never feel close to people (20 percent) or feel like there are people they can talk to (18 percent). These stats do not suggest people don't have any friends whatsoever, but that they lack *close* friends. They may have friends to shoot the breeze with and have a good time over a holiday weekend, but they're not *close* to them. They're not known by them. They don't depend on each other when the going gets tough. Maybe they don't want to appear weak or convey that they "need" others. But I think it's more likely they just don't know *how* to be weak and lean into their God-given need for others. They're afraid they'll scare off their friends with that level of vulnerability.

Perhaps our loneliness epidemic isn't due to having no friends whatsoever, although there are certainly instances of that. Rather, could it be due to not having close friends to support our interdependent design in the wake of an independent culture? We just don't know how to get close.

WE NEED CLOSER FRIENDS

Robin Dunbar became famous when he discovered that 150 appears to be the magic number for the maximum amount of friends we can maintain at once, which has since been deemed "Dunbar's Number."[64] Within these 150 relationships are layers of friendships with varying levels of depth and intimacy. Each layer in the diagram of Dunbar's number includes the category of friends in its subsequent layers, so it can be broken down as follows:

- 100 friends
- 35 good friends

- 10 best friends
- 3 close friends
- 1–2 intimate friends

Add them all together, and you get 150 friends.

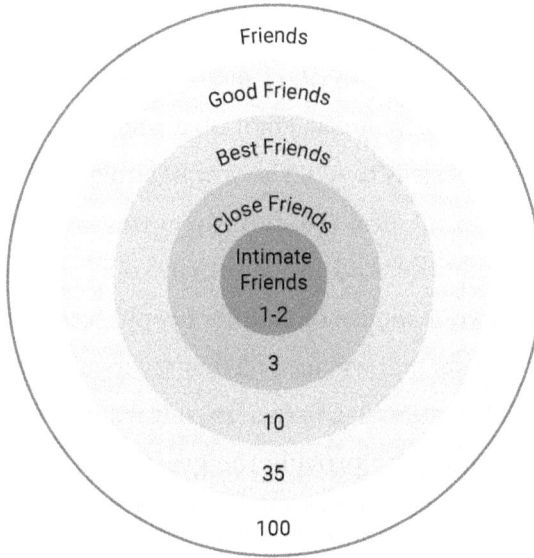

Dunbar's Number

The one-hundred-friends layer includes your casual friends. These are the people you'd invite to your wedding, a funeral, or some other one-time life event that you'd like them to attend. They're weak ties you still maintain through social media from past seasons of life, but they're not the ones you're going to call to help you pack up boxes and help you move across town.

The next layer includes fifty "good friends." These are the friends who bring you pleasure and joy. They're the ones you would likely invite to a graduation party, your birthday dinner, or a Fourth of July BBQ, attend classes with, and share a decent conversation with when you run into them at the local coffee shop.

But within this fifty-person layer of friends is a subset of up to fifteen "best friends." These are people you have strong ties with. You provide emotional support for each other, rush over to give each other eggs needed for a recipe, help each other with house projects, go on vacations together, and all-around share deeper parts of yourselves with each other.

Finally, within this fifteen-friend layer are your five "close" and "intimate" friends. These are the friends whose shoulders you can cry on. They provide financial, emotional, and physical help when the going gets especially tough. They're not afraid to see you at your worst, and you're not afraid to show them yourself at your worst. You happily rely and depend on each other. Your "intimate" friends, then, are either your spouse or another deeply personal friend.[65]

Dunbar suggests that we need all four layers of relationships to experience full relational satisfaction, but it's our ten "best" and five "close" friends who provide the greatest sense of support, connection, belonging, and relational well-being. The problem is the majority of Americans have no close or intimate friends who fully know them and love them as they are.[66] This falls in line with the stats that say people are hungering for closer friendships that they can depend on.

In my own research, interviewees reported that the top source of receiving support came from their friends. Four specifically mentioned support coming from "close friends" or their "inner circle," while other mentions included roommates, classmates, or just friends in general. My interviewees also identified specific ways that friends help them feel supported, which included

- **Honesty/Vulnerability:** talking about anything, not having to sugarcoat anything, having rant sessions to "get everything out," and trusting their friends.
- **Commonalities:** doing hobbies together, sharing similar life

goals and passions, sharing common deeper meaning and goals with their faith, and relating to common experiences.

- **Conversation:** having constant communication about their lives, having someone to share their lives with, just talking and offering encouragement and advice.
- **Listening:** having someone there to listen to them and being seen or heard.

Additionally, 50 percent of my interviewees' responses to the question, "Do you hunger for anything deeper about your friendships?" pertained to sharing deeply about personal matters, like having a friend who is always available to talk in times of need, talking about a struggle that's difficult to share, having conversation where nothing is off limits, and having a deeper understanding of each other. A lot of what they described lines up with the characteristics of Dunbar's descriptions of "intimate," "close," and "best friends."

———

Mother Theresa, a saint of the Catholic church who is known for her work with serving those in poverty, once said, "I have seen the starving. But in your country, I have seen an even greater hunger. That is the hunger to be loved. No place in all of my travels have I seen such loneliness as I have seen in the poverty of affluence in America." Drawing closer to our friends ultimately comes from a willingness to be interdependent, not independent. But until we're willing to give up the image of not being weak, overcome the fear of disclosing the hard parts of our lives to others, and go against our individualist mantra by declaring that "we need friends," our loneliness epidemic will carry on.

But there's another side to our loneliness coin. Not only do we live in an individualist culture that declares we don't need anyone else, but we also live in an isolationist culture that declares, "We don't *want* anyone else."

DISCUSSION QUESTIONS

1. What sticks out to you the most about the difference between collectivist cultures and individualist cultures?

2. What are the benefits of living in an individualist culture?

3. What are some of the drawbacks to living in an individualist culture? How do you see them hindering our ability to live in relationship?

4. Why do you think people are so hesitant to say they "need anyone else"? Have there been times when you fell into a similar mind-set?

5. What are some things you can do to push back against our individualistic culture and rely on other people more?

CHAPTER 4

"I DON'T WANT ANYONE ELSE"

Unfriendly people care only about themselves;
they lash out at common sense.

– Proverbs 18:1 –

Prior to the 1950s, American culture looked much like human civilization had for centuries. People's homes, retail stores, and workplaces were all within walking distance. Houses were built tall and skinny, so they could be close to one another for optimal space, and placed near the roads for easy access. But at the front of these homes was the icon for American social life: the front porch.[67]

Front porches were considered a "public square" of sorts, where neighbors could hang out and shoot the breeze on their way to work or in the evenings to wind down after a long day. It was an area where people from the closely packed community could easily interact with one another at their leisure.[68]

The front porch: the icon of America's social landscape.

But after World War II, America's social landscape began to change. People started flocking to suburban neighborhoods for cheaper land and less congested living conditions than those found in the inner city. As the suburban-style home became more popular, the front porch was replaced with tiny walkways, large garages, and a front lawn that pulled the house away from the sidewalk. New building codes saw front porches as unnecessary expenses, whereas garages and driveways for people's individualized means of transportation became essential. Eventually, the garage door opener came along, enabling people to open and close their garages without even needing to get out of their cars. As convenient as an invention as it was, the garage door opener also enabled people to enter their home without even saying a word to their neighbors.

Then another game-changing invention came along that served as another nail in the coffin of the front porch: air conditioning. Now people could just stay inside their homes where it can be cooled to a comfortable seventy-one degrees during the hottest days of summer, eliminating the need even to be outside at all, let alone socialize on a front porch. Finally, the front porch, which once served as the public square for neighbors to socialize regularly with each other, was replaced with the back porch, surrounded by a picket fence, so families could still enjoy the outdoors but in isolation from their neighbors.

The style of modern suburban homes, with the front porch replaced with a garage and small entrance.

Modern-day architecture has made homes less like public squares and more like isolated fortresses. Skye Jethani again offers his observations to this phenomenon when he says,

> Most homes are set as far back from public spaces, the street and sidewalk, as possible. The rooms facing the street tend to be the spaces we use least—the formal living room or dining

room. The spaces where real life happens, the kitchen and family room, are hidden in the back. Outdoor recreation is also confined to the back of the house, usually behind a fence. Everything about suburban home design communicates to the passerby, "Leave me alone!"[69]

When was the last time you talked to your neighbors? I barely know all the names of my own. And to be entirely honest, there's a part of me that hesitates to get to know much else about them beyond their names. I, personally, suffer from the American value of isolationism myself.

While our individualism declares, "I don't need anyone else," our cultural value of isolationism declares "I don't want anyone else." We want to be alone, withdraw from our social contexts, and pursue our cozy, individualistic lives, rid of people we don't want to interact with, from our isolated fortresses we call "homes."

Although many of us won't come right out and say we don't want anyone else, it's certainly implied as a preference when you look at our newfound isolationist tendencies that extend beyond the architecture of our homes. The examples abound. Services like Amazon Prime can deliver anything you want—even groceries—to your door in less than two days (sometimes in two *hours*, depending on where you live). You don't even have to leave the comfort of your home, let alone interact with Walmart employees to help you find where the peanut butter powder is located. And even if you are shopping at Walmart, you can just look up where the peanut butter powder is located on their app (because let's face it, we're terrified or too lazy to ask for help).

Or take online clothing subscription services like Stitch Fix. They can send you a new, fresh, "trendy" outfit every month without you ever having to ask for an employee's help at an American Eagle Outfitters. This is a *godsend* for people like me, because I utterly despise the process of shopping for new clothes. Seriously. Asking another human being to open up a changing room so I can try on a bunch of new clothes is in my top ten of "most awkward interactions I could ever have with others" list. But again, this online service robs me of the opportunity to interact with other human beings by moving an activity that would be done with the help of others to the comfort of my home, by myself.

Or how about Carvana? This online service allows you to shop for a car *all on your phone*, without ever interacting with another human being. Fast-food chains like McDonalds have massive touch screens for you to tap the specifics of your order, all while spending three times longer placing it, but it's worth it because you don't have to interact with a person at the register. Order ahead on your Starbucks app, Taco Bell app, Subway app—any restaurant app, for that matter—so you just have to pop in and out without even saying a word to anybody. You're not just "skipping the line"—you're skipping interacting with people.

More and more education models are moving online, where you pursue your degree through videos, readings, and assignments done on your own initiative without a classroom or in-person classmates. Online gaming has moved socializing from exploring the outdoors with your friends after school to sitting alone in your basement while talking with your friends over a headset. Movie theaters are on their last leg of their life span, as COVID popularized watching new movies on their sponsored streaming services from the comfort of moviegoers' homes instead of with friends in front of the big screen. Hate sitting on an airplane with a bunch of strangers? Now you can put on an Apple Vision Pro and magically make all your surroundings disappear while you watch your favorite episodes of

Friends on a giant, private, virtual screen displayed in your over-priced computerized goggles.

As much as all these services save you the inconvenience of having to go to the store or waiting till *Friends* plays at 4:00 p.m. on TBS, they also rob you of the opportunity to interact with real human beings. Because community is uncomfortable, friendship is burdensome, and the omnipresence of the internet allows for instant entertainment on a whim, it is far too easy to retreat to isolated lifestyles of personal consumption and comfort, stripped from community and significant friendships, all while safely, and emotionally, barricaded in our homes. Why would we even want anyone else to provide for our needs?

Isolationism is a heck of a lot more comfortable. But it all comes at a cost. The discomfort of social interaction is traded for the discomfort of loneliness and decreased socializing abilities. But instead of remedying our loneliness with *friends*, as God intended, we numb it with more and more isolated entertainment and media consumption. And, as you can probably tell from the common thread of all the examples I just gave, perhaps no tool has fueled our newfound isolationist lifestyles more than the smartphone and social media.

ENTER THE IPHONE

January 9, 2007, was just another ordinary day in the world. But little did the world know it was about to change drastically.

Steve Jobs, the CEO of Apple at the time, took the stage for a keynote presentation at the Macworld Conference. After the initial reports of how the company was faring, Jobs paused, then said, "This is a day I've been looking forward to for a very long time." He announced that Apple would be releasing three brand-new products:

1. A widescreen iPod with touch controls
2. A revolutionary mobile phone
3. A breakthrough internet communication device

But the catch was that these weren't three separate devices. They were *one* device. And that one device was none other than the iPhone.

You can probably imagine how ecstatic I was as an Apple sheep watching this keynote address. I—and the rest of the world—were floored. Never before had such a device hit the market. And I knew I had to get it. So, on June 28, 2007, my mom and I hit the road to Muncie, Indiana, and camped outside an AT&T store to ensure that we would get the device (seriously, coolest mom *ever*). We weren't the only ones; we met some dear friends that day who also wanted to get their hands on this revolutionary product. It involved twenty-four long hours of sleeping in our cars, sitting in the rain, eating fast food, and doing everything we could to keep ourselves entertained (remember, we didn't have smartphones to do that yet; instead, I had to play Bejeweled on my mom's PalmPilot). Well, to our dismay, it turned out we could've arrived merely three hours before the release time and still gotten one—but I wouldn't have traded this experience for the world! I remember the AT&T store opening, working our way through the partition lines, and getting my hands on my very first iPhone . . .

And I've been an iPhone user ever since.

The iPhone ushered in a communication revolution that has completely transformed how the world interacts, operates, and relates with each other. Just over half a century ago, to communicate with someone in another country required countless days waiting for letters to be delivered back and forth between parties. Now, it is as simple as pressing a video icon on a phone to see their face in the palm of your hand while being thousands of miles away. We can now google up locations of local coffee shops and get turn-by-turn directions in a new city without looking at a physical map or printing off directions from MapQuest. Instead of putting in a disc on a DVD player to watch a movie, we can just stream it on our phones. Instead of using car keys to start our cars, we can press a button on an app from hundreds of feet away. Don't want to get up to change the thermostat of your house? Just do it through your smart home app. Why carry around a separate DSLR camera to document your life when your phone can take nearly as good of photos and videos? And don't even get me started on the breakthrough technology behind Snapchat filters!

Perhaps the most profound innovation of the smartphone, though, was how it brought about an entirely new means for us to interact via social media. Little did we know what social media could become in the early days of the smartphone.

NOT-SO-SOCIAL MEDIA

The initial iteration of social media was great; the posts, likes, comments, messaging, and sharing abilities certainly served as great *supplements* to friendships. But the problem has arisen where people are using social media as the *substitute* for real, in-person friendships. I once heard someone say that our interactions on social media are more with phantoms than they are with real individuals. While there are some who will vulnerably post about the struggles going on in their lives, that is typically an exception to the rule. Social media literally gives everyone the power to create their own customized identity, whether it is to show off the highlight reel of their lives, make up stories to come across as more "impressive" than what they perceive themselves to be, and at worst, create fake persons entirely. So really, it's debatable if we interact with people's real, authentic selves online in the first place.

The deeper issue, though, as Skye Jethani points out in his book *The Divine Commodity*, is that more and more young people are utilizing social media as the sole mediator of their social engagements with other people. "Rather than encouraging healthy relationships with real people, these sites foster pseudo-relationships through shallow identities."[70] Author, businessman, and leadership guru Simon Sinek writes on similar findings in his book *Leaders Eat Last*. He explains that many use social media as their prime relationship mediator because online relationships *feel* real. When we receive texts via iMessage, rack up likes on a clever Facebook post or major life update, accumulate more followers on Instagram, or video chat with someone across the state, our brains release the same chemicals associated with social engagements—but only in bursts. He says, "Put simply, though the love may feel real, the relationship is still virtual. Relationships can certainly start online, but they only become real when we meet face-to-face."[71]

Sinek makes the point that if social media is the be-all and end-all for all human relationships, then why is it always better to experience a concert in person than watching it on YouTube? Why is it sometimes better to sit in the nosebleed section at a live NBA game despite having a better view on ESPN in your living room? Why go to a movie theater when you can just watch a film on your iPhone in bed? Why purchase groceries at the store when Amazon delivers them to your door? And, ultimately, why is it better to spend time with friends in person than online? It's because the purest essence of the human experience happens when we're together, in person, interacting *face-to-face*. It's embedded into the God-given design of our biology, and no technological revolution can change that. Yet more and more of us are spending less and less time in person and face-to-face. This is especially the case for Gen Zers, who are considered our loneliest generation today. And the connection between Gen Zers' decrease in face time and increase in loneliness may be stronger than we think.[72]

THE GREAT REWIRING OF CHILDHOOD

Jonathan Haidt, the moral psychologist, who said, as I shared in chapter 2, that we are at our happiest when we are immersed in significant relationships, wrote perhaps the most important book of our lifetime, called *The Anxious Generation*, about social media, smartphones, and their impact on the mental health crisis among today's young people. He proposes that the high rates of anxiety, depression, suicide attempts, self-harm, and loneliness among teens and young adults are due to a major shift from a play-based childhood to a phone-based childhood, which he calls "the Great Rewiring of Childhood."[73] This shift began as early as the late 1980s but culminated when the smartphone became widely adopted between 2010 and 2015. In a play-based childhood, kids were freer to explore and discover the real world with their peers with a higher sense of independence that produced higher risk resilience when they became adults. But in a phone-based childhood, Haidt claims kids are being overprotected in the real world while being underprotected in the virtual world. Instead of playing outside and spending time with friends, they are remaining sedentary inside with unmonitored screen time, taking fewer risks, and not socializing face-to-face with their peers and family. He says,

> With so many new and exciting virtual activities, many adolescents (and adults) lost the ability to be fully present with the people around them, which changed social life for everyone, even for the small minority that did not use these platforms.

That is why I refer to the period from 2010 to 2015 as the Great Rewiring of Childhood. Social patterns, role models, emotions, physical activity, and even sleep patterns were fundamentally recast, for adolescents, over the course of just five years.[74]

A NEW DRUG

Around the same time the smartphone became widely adopted into mainstream culture, social media apps started changing their designs to become much more addictive. We are currently living in an age that the advertising world calls "The Attention Economy," where the longer companies and brands can hold your attention, the more money they make. This incentivizes developers of apps like Facebook, Instagram, YouTube, Snapchat, Tinder, and many of the other apps we regularly use, to design apps with algorithms that intentionally exploit our psychology. Dopamine releases into our brains with every notification, like, and comment, while delivering us content perfectly curated to fit our personality and interests.[75] That's why it feels so good every time you get a new notification. But it's also what keeps us coming back to these apps again and again for more and more, getting more dopamine hits, unconsciously spending hours on them, all the while being subtly exposed to advertisements that make these businesses even more money (and who certainly do not care about your well-being).

Tristan Harries, who once worked as an ethicist for Google, notes how the apps and devices designed by Google, Apple, and Facebook were limiting our attention spans for anything else beyond screens:

> In an attention economy, there's only so much attention and the advertising business model always wants more. So, it becomes a race to the bottom of the brainstem. . . . It starts small. First to get your attention, I add slot machine "pull to refresh" rewards which create little addictions. I remove stopping cues for

"infinite scroll" so your mind forgets when to do something else. But then that's not enough. As attention gets more competitive, we have to crawl deeper down the brainstem to your identity and get you addicted to getting attention from other people. By adding the number of followers and likes, technology hacks our social validation and now people are obsessed with the constant feedback they get from others. This helped fuel a mental health crisis for teenagers.[76]

What doesn't help the addictive nature of these apps is how deeply personal they are. Our social media consumption directly contributes to our identity, values, and sense of self, all thanks to their algorithms that curate newsfeeds tailored to our unique interests. Since our individualism values the freedom to be whoever we want to be, we "follow" (or, more accurately, "consume") the content, ideas, and people that reinforce our elected identities. However, whatever social media chooses to expose us to can over time inform our sense of identity, whether we seek it out or not. Social media use is a driving force for our individualism and identity formation, for better or for worse, whether we want it to be or not.[77] So how could we *not* spend all this time on these devices if they reinforce so much of who we are and play into our social validation? They are such a core part of our lives, in fact, that we can even suffer withdrawal symptoms, like anxiety, irritability, and FOBO (fear of being offline) if removed from these devices that provide a steady stream of dopamine releases to our brains every day.[78]

Why does this matter? The addictive nature of these devices and services is so consequential to our design for community because they increase our screen time while decreasing our face time.

INCREASED SCREEN TIME MEANS DECREASED FACE TIME

Barna, a Christian-based research and statistics firm, found that typical 15-to-23-year-olds spend 2,767 hours on screen media each year. That is roughly 115 days of *not* being with others, doing recreational activities, or even sleeping.[79] One study found Gen Z high school seniors spend an average of six hours a day with digital media, which includes texting, browsing the internet, video gaming, and video calling,[80] whereas another study marks that number anywhere between six to eight hours per day.[81]

For prior generations, hanging out with friends daily after school was commonplace. In 1991, about 55 percent of boys and 45 percent of girls said they meet up with their friends outside of school "almost every day." That number was on a steady decrease to 42 percent and 39 percent for boys and girls, respectively, by 2010, but then decreased sharply to about 30 percent of boys and 25 percent of girls who met up with their friends daily by 2017.[82] That means today's young people spend almost 50 percent less time interacting with peers face-to-face than those even fifteen years ago.[83] Of course, this doesn't mean young people don't socialize at all. They just socialize *differently* than previous generations, primarily now through digital means. Teens and young adults are more likely to socialize with their friends over FaceTime, online gaming, or social media as their primary form of social interaction. Seventy-five percent of them use Snapchat, Instagram, YouTube, and Facebook on a daily basis.[84] So, rather than going to people's houses or a third space like a coffee shop to socialize like generations past, Gen Zers return to the "isolated fortresses" of their homes and interact with friends online.[85]

The irony in this trend is we're socializing while isolated. We're together, but alone. The truth is not all connections are created equal. Social media isn't so much connecting with friends as it is consuming friends' content while isolated in "digital bubbles."[86] It *feels* like connection—but it's not. One hundred and fifteen days spent on a screen is still 115 days not engaging in relationships face-to-face. Although social media increases the *quantity* of social connections, it consequently reduces the *quality* of those connections. Haidt says,

> When everything moved onto smartphones in the early 2010s, both girls and boys experienced a gigantic increase in the number of their social ties and in the time required to service these ties (such as reading and commenting on the posts of acquaintances or maintaining dozes of Snapchat "streaks" with people who are not your closest friends). This explosive growth necessarily caused a decline in the number and depth of close friendships.[87]

This relates back to Dunbar's work on the four circles of friendships. He says that the time we allot to one friend is time that can't be given to others, and the more time we devote to certain friends ultimately determines their quality and value in our life. Dunbar estimates that we spend 40 percent of our social bandwidth on our five close-intimate friends and 20 percent on our ten best friends. That means our fifteen closest friends get 60 percent of our social effort and the time needed for that.[88] But what happens if the time needed to invest in these close friends is invested through supremely more insufficient means, like social media, instead? If relational satisfaction comes down to maintaining deep, intimate, personal, close friendships, then we are prohibiting ourselves from investing in those closer friendships by spending more time on these addictive, superficial, digital connections. We may be "connecting," sure—but we're doing so while isolated. And it only furthers the consequences of the loneliness epidemic on our God-given design for community.

SCREENS' IMPACT ON OUR DESIGN FOR COMMUNITY

1. Lessened In-Personal Social Abilities. While we young people may tout that we do "better on a screen than face-to-face with others," it clearly comes with its drawbacks.[89] Heavy screen use and media consumption alter our physiology and social skills, particularly during our formative teen years. Due to the neuroplasticity of the brain, technology can affect thought processes, emotions, dreams, memory, attention spans, reading habits, and sleep cycles.[90] One study found that children who engaged in more than seven hours of screen time a day experienced a thinning of their brain's cortex, the part of the brain that develops critical thinking and reasoning.[91] Extensive digital socialization at the expense of face-to-face interaction leads to higher relational deficiencies and lack of social development, such as losing the "ability to recognize and respond to facial cues, voice tone and inflection, body language, and the energy of emotions in the room."[92]

Our screen time even impacts how we relate with each other in person. When we're with our friends, so are our smartphones. When we sit around the table, our phones are right there, too, resting on the table as we eat lunch, or our smart watches tap us with incoming notifications on our wrists as we talk. And when we address those notifications in those moments, we shift our attention away from the conversation we're having with our friends to whatever is on our screens. This ever so subtly communicates that what's on my screen is more important than you. We have lost the ability to give people our fully undivided attention. So even in those brief moments of reading a text, we isolate ourselves from those gathered right in our midst by shutting down our presence and attention. We're near them, but we're not *with* them.

Given all this, it shouldn't be a surprise that overusing screens for communication means underusing in-person social skills, which naturally yields deficient in-person relationships, lower relational satisfaction, and increased loneliness.

2. Increased Loneliness. Some suggest social media's influence on loneliness is more a matter of correlation than causation, in that people who are already lonely correlate to increased social media use, rather than social media causing their loneliness.[93] While that is true in some cases, these conclusions are based on analyzing the general public's social media habits, not just those of one generation who prefers connecting with their communities over a screen.[94] Jen Twenge, who is known for her groundbreaking research on Gen Z in her book iGen, found that teens and young adults who regularly visit social media sites each day "are more likely to agree [with the statements] 'I often feel lonely,' 'I feel left out of things,' and 'I often wish I had more good friends.' . . . In contrast, those who spend time with their friends in person or who play sports are less lonely."[95] Again, if more time is spent online, then there's less time available to be with friends in person, and loneliness and its side effects ensue—such as worsened mental health.

3. Worsened Mental Health. We've already learned that loneliness worsens mental health conditions, but excessive social media use and screen time just throw even more fuel on the fire. More and more studies are showing that heavy social media users are more likely to suffer from depression, anxiety, and other mental health disorders than light users,[96] and are consequently more likely to disconnect socially under such mental health conditions.[97] One way social media proliferates worsened mental health conditions is through FOMO: the fear of missing out. Seeing what our friends are doing on social media without us can be an isolating experience, making us feel like we're on the fringes of our friends' inner circle. The concept of FOMO can even be seen as a form of social rejection and exclusivity.[98] Susan Mettes comments,

People who have a problem with FOMO often agree with statements like "I get anxious when I don't know what my friends are up to" and "I fear others have more rewarding experiences than me." They tend to use social media more frequently than other people do. Fear of missing out might seem laughable, but it's a form of distress.[99]

4. Pornography Addiction. Finally, beneath the already absurd amount of evidence that our phones fight against our design for community is another digitally isolating habit that hardly ever gets talked about, and it only furthers our sense of loneliness: pornography addiction. Teens and young adults view porn more than anyone else, with college students between the ages of eighteen and twenty-four viewing it the most.[100] Our smartphones have made pornography both more accessible and addictive than ever before. Extensive porn use not only affects the brain the same way addictive drugs and tobacco do, but it also elicits deeper feelings of loneliness.[101] One study found that "the association between loneliness and viewing pornography was positive [i.e., related] and significant. . . . Those who viewed pornography were more likely to experience loneliness, and those who were experiencing loneliness were more likely to view pornography."[102]

Since excessive porn consumption can yield feelings of shame, guilt, and self-condemnation, people are more likely to conceal the habit and keep it a secret. However, withholding this habit in secret only further isolates them from friends, partners, and loved ones who can aid them in difficult times. Confessing a porn addiction is not the easiest thing to do, even with trusted and caring friends and loved ones. The worse someone feels about himself, the more likely he is to seek comfort from porn, which makes him feel even worse about himself, lessening the likelihood of confessing it to others, driving him further into loneliness, seeking porn to comfort himself, and on and on and on the cycle goes.[103] Perhaps this is the most contorted form of our God-given design for community and intimacy with others. Instead of reserving sex as the deepest form of intimacy experienced between a husband and wife, people isolate themselves for a pseudo form of this intimacy with a stranger on a screen. It may give them pleasure, but it leaves them alone and numb.

Truly, it appears that social media isn't so social after all.

"AND THEN WE WILL TALK FACE-TO-FACE"

There's an itty bitty book in the Bible called 3 John. Coming in at only fifteen verses long, it's a short letter written by the apostle John to a fellow church leader and dear friend named Gaius. John praises Gaius for all the hospitality he's been providing for traveling teachers of the gospel, and gives a couple other warnings and encouragement along the way. But at the end of the letter, John writes these words: "I have much more to say to you, but I don't want to write it with pen and ink. For I hope to see you soon, and then we will talk face to face" (3 John 13–14).

Perhaps no other passage in Scripture cuts more to the heart of what we need right now in our isolated, digital age.

We have so much we want to say to people, but unlike John, we insist on writing it with pen and ink. Or, more accurately, we write it with text and emojis through iMessage, text messages, email, slack, Instagram DMs—what have you. I think it's safe to agree when Haidt says, "The Great Rewiring devastated the social lives of Gen Z by connecting them to everyone in the world and disconnecting them from the people around them."[104] Although smartphones and social media particularly affect Gen Z and young adults, the truth is we have *all* fallen into this isolationist trap where we would rather be on our phones than with others. If people substitute high-quality, in-person human interaction with low-quality, digital interaction, their ability to connect with others will suffer. On one hand, social media can certainly be a tool that supplements how we interact with our friends. I have no doubt that John and Gaius would've hopped on a FaceTime call to catch up if they were given the choice two thousand years ago. But there's a crucial difference between Face-Time and face time. On the other hand, social media can deepen loneliness if it excessively substitutes in-person interaction. Some may even say our newsfeeds have become a new digital form of the "front porch." But it's not even close to being the same as what our country's social landscape once was.

I think we all would be way better off if we could learn how to put our phones down and say, "I hope to see you soon so we can talk face-to-face." Doing so would help us fight against the isolationist mantra of "I don't want anyone else" by saying, instead, "I *do* want you." We need to learn how to choose our friends, to see them, and to deem them as so much more important to us than anything else our cozy, individualistic, isolated lifestyles offer us. Community and friendship require much more effort, but they are far more satisfying. Shared, in-person social experiences teach us how to interact with our peers, observe their body language, communicate effectively, build social resilience against rejection, and strengthen our identity formation, because they satisfy our design for community.[105]

THE LONELINESS EPIDEMIC: IN SUM

It's not good to be alone. God designed us to feel loneliness as the "check engine" light for our need for community. When utilized properly, loneliness is an invitation for us to reach out and befriend others. But when left unchecked, extended periods of loneliness wreak havoc on our bodies, minds, and souls. Conversely, the very nature of our God is communal. He is a community of three persons: the Father, Son, and Holy Spirit. Therefore, Adam was not fully made into the image of God until God created Eve for them both to live in community with God, where each could be fully known with nothing to hide. This is why our quality of life dramatically increases in virtually every aspect when we are connected in meaningful community with God and others, as we were originally designed.

However, while sin is on its last dying breath, it does still have its grip on this world. One of the schemes of the enemy is to keep us isolated and alone, and he has taken advantage of our cultural values of individualism and isolationism, using them to drive us further apart from one another and deeper into loneliness. Now we're left believing the lies that we don't need anyone else and that we don't want anyone else.

But deep down, we *know* that we do. We are desperate for community, love, and belonging. We need friends who know us, care for us, and are there for us *in person.* There has got to be another way to live this friendless, disconnected, isolated life.

Thank God, there is. But . . .

If we are to reclaim our design for community with God and each other in our modern era, then we need to navigate our friendships and lifestyles in an entirely different way. A *deeper* way. A way that emphasizes our need for others, prioritizing their role in our lives, which forms us more into who God has called us to be, while drawing us closer to him and each other. Our path for moving forward, though, begins by looking *backward* at how the church has historically addressed this issue. The solution for our loneliness epidemic, then, is surprisingly found in a long-lost Christian doctrine and practice, called spiritual friendship, that needs to be resurrected.

And it all starts with befriending the most important person we could ever possibly befriend, for it is from his friendship we truly learn how to be friends with others as God intended.

DISCUSSION QUESTIONS

1. What specific technology advancement has made your life more comfortable at the expense of interacting with others (for example, ordering ahead at fast-food restaurants, ordering from Amazon Prime, watching movies at home instead of the theater, etc.)?
2. How have you particularly experienced the isolating tendencies that a smartphone and social media bring into your life?
3. What does a healthy use of technology and social media look like, where it can enhance relationships rather than replace them?
4. What are some boundaries you can put in place that can help you decrease your screen time on your phone and increase your face time with others?

PART II

SPIRITUAL FRIENDSHIP

CHAPTER 5

JESUS IS A FRIEND OF YOURS

I no longer call you servants . . .
Instead, I have called you friends.

– John 15:15 (NIV) –

I wish I could be friends with Chris Pratt.

Chris is one of my favorite actors of all time. I was first drawn to him from his impeccable performance as Andy Dwyer in *Parks and Recreation*. His nuttiness and spunk won the hearts of many, and it's what ultimately helped him land other landmark acting roles like Star Lord in *Guardians of the Galaxy*, Owen Grady in *Jurassic World*, and—most notably—Emmett the Construction Worker in *The LEGO Movie* (which is the best animated film of all time, by the way).

Chris Pratt is incredibly successful, funny, and charismatic. I can't help but wonder what doing life with Chris Pratt would look like. If we could FaceTime on a whim, text throughout the day, hang out at his multimillion-dollar mansion, and build LEGO sets while binge-watching *Parks and Recreation*.

But of course, I'm not friends with Chris Pratt, and chances are very, very low that I will *ever* be friends with Chris Pratt. That's simply due to the fact of who Chris Pratt *is*. He's on a whole other level of celebrity status than me, which greatly increases the distance between my status and his. There's the whole security issue—how close would his bodyguards even let me get? Even if I had the chance to meet him, I'd maybe get an autograph at least, but I would only be viewed as a fan of his, not a friend.

As much as I would love to be friends with Chris Pratt, there are just far too many legitimate reasons that hinder that friendship from ever happening.

Maybe you have similar feelings about people you wish you could be friends with, like Peyton Manning, or Taylor Swift, or Joey Tribiani from *Friends*, or Nelson Mandela, or the Greek philosopher Aristotle. We all have an infinite amount of reasons we wish we could be friends with these people. But the very fact we *wish* we could be friends with them shines a blinding light on all the reasons we *can't* be friends with them, whether that's due to the difference in status, distance, or if they're even real (let alone alive). As amazing as it sounds, we're grounded in the reality that we can never befriend people of such high status and renown.

I think we tend to view being friends with God the same way.

Being friends with God is an ideal we'd love to achieve, but perhaps feel that in reality he would never allow such a friendship to exist. Just like how we feel about befriending celebrities or historical figures, we can know a lot *about* God, and even be "in tune" with what he's doing by going to church, reading Scripture, following other spiritual leaders on social media, and so forth. But if that's the fullest expression of our friendship with God, then that's as shallow as following LeBron James or Christ Pratt or Beyonce on Instagram and thinking we're best friends with them.

What does it truly mean to be friends with God? And why do we have such a hard time with it?

TO BEFRIEND THE LORD

It was just like any other Passover celebration. Jesus was gathered with his twelve disciples to celebrate this holiday, enjoying a good meal in remembrance of when God delivered the Hebrews from slavery in Egypt. But the night took an unexpected turn for the worse when Jesus disclosed that he was about to be betrayed and handed over to be killed.

This naturally led to an outcry from his disciples, despite Jesus alluding this day would come on many different occasions through-out his three years of ministry with them. "Who would do such a thing?" they asked. "Surely it's not me, Lord!" (Matthew 26:22, author's paraphrase). After Jesus revealed that Judas would indeed betray him, Judas leaves the upper room to put his plans in motion.

Obviously, the disciples would've been very distraught. That's why, according to John's Gospel, John spends *five chapters* in scrip-ture, John 13–17, sharing what's known as Jesus's "farewell address." In these chapters, Jesus encourages his disciples, reveals his plans for why this has to occur, and how they will relate with him in the future. One excerpt from this address includes a radically new way for the disciples to view their relationship with their Rabbi. Here's what Jesus says in John 15:9–17:

> As the Father has loved me, so have I loved you. Now remain in
> my love. If you keep my commands, you will remain in my love,
> just as I have kept my Father's commands and remain in his love.
> I have told you this so that my joy may be in you and that your joy
> may be complete. My command is this: Love each other as I have
> loved you. Greater love has no one than this: to lay down one's
> life for one's friends. You are my friends if you do what I com-
> mand. I no longer call you servants, because a servant does not
> know his master's business. Instead, I have called you friends,
> for everything that I learned from my Father I have made known
> to you. You did not choose me, but I chose you and appointed
> you so that you might go and bear fruit—fruit that will last—and
> so that whatever you ask in my name the Father will give you.
> This is my command: Love each other. (NIV)

This would've knocked the socks off the disciples' feet.

They had spent the last three years following Jesus all across ancient Palestine as their Rabbi, ministering alongside him, healing the sick, and gleaning everything he had ever taught. One of the principles they heard Jesus teach over and over again was what's known as the Great Reversal: To become great, you must become the least.[106] Strive not to be served, but to serve. The last will be first, and the first will be last. Deny yourself, pick up your cross, and follow Jesus.

All that to say, Jesus drilled the importance of servanthood into the disciples' minds, both in terms of how they relate to others and in how they relate to God. They were *servants*.

But what would have been so puzzling to the disciples was when Jesus says in John 15:15, "I no longer call you servants, because a servant does not know his master's business. Instead, I have called you friends, for everything that I have learned from my Father I have made known to you."

It appears, as author Brian Edgar aptly notes, that Jesus just invoked the Great Reversal of the Great Reversal.[107] "I no longer call you servants . . . Instead, I have called you friends."

Just when the disciples were finally getting this service thing down and embracing this upside-down way to live, Jesus flips it all on its head *again*. They are no longer servants of Jesus. They are *friends* of Jesus. This is a radically different kind of relationship with their Lord than they ever imagined.

And honestly? It's just about as radical for us.

A NEW WAY TO RELATE WITH GOD

We often talk in church circles about how Christianity isn't a religion, but a relationship. Our faith isn't about checking off boxes and following a bunch of rules, but how we can be in relationship with our Almighty God. But have we ever paused to ask, What kind of a relationship with God are we even talking about? Do we even know? For whatever reason, we keep that relationship with God broad and ambiguous: it's just a "relationship." But that's not how our earthly relationships work.

In regard to all our relationships, we assign titles to them so we know exactly *how* to relate and behave with them, like "mom," "dad," "brother," "sister," "spouse," "boss," "coworker," "teacher," "president," "CEO," and even "friend." These titles are important, because I guarantee that you don't relate with your mom the same way you do with the bros in your fraternity, and you probably don't say the same things about your workplace environment to your boss as you do with your coworkers during lunch hour. Titles give us a framework for how we speak, dress, and behave within these relationships. The same is true with God. Therefore, it's important to recognize the different titles we assign to God, because those titles directly determine how we relate and interact with him.

In his book, *God Is Friendship*, Brian Edgar refers to this concept as metaphoric theology. He says, "Metaphoric theology is the analysis of the various images and metaphors used for God and the way they function as attempts to name God and to describe the relationship of God with humanity."[108] Put simply, it is impossible to fully comprehend who God is because he exists beyond what our human imaginations are able to process. Therefore, metaphoric theology is our attempt to describe who God is, what he does, and who we are in human terms that our measly little brains can understand (despite our terms still falling infinitely short).

The following table lists some of these metaphors (or "titles") we assign to God, the titles we receive in relation to each title of God, and the consequent actions we do within each relationship.

Relational Titles for God	Our Relationship to That Title	How We Relate to That Title
God	Human	Worship
Creator	Creation	Live according to his design
Lord	Servant	Serve and obey his will
Leader	Follower	Follow his guidance and direction
Teacher	Student	Learn from his teachings and wisdom
Master	Apprentice	Live by his example
Father	Son/Daughter	Covered by his loving protection
King	Civilian	Abide by his decrees

If you've been a Christian for a while, you've most likely heard God referred to by these titles. But do you notice a common thread in all of them? They are all *vertical relationships*. They position God in a hierarchy, where God is *above us* in some way. This is similar to vertical relationships in our own life, like our bosses, professors, governing authorities, and parents. But what these vertical relationships with God demonstrate is how drastically different we are as humans in comparison to the Almighty God of the universe. It's a comparison between two beings of completely different status. One is supreme, perfect, divine, sovereign, and infinite, and the other is poor, imperfect, humane, and finite. So it's only natural that the lesser must serve the greater. The civilian *must* abide by the king's decrees, the student *must* learn from the teacher, the follower *must* follow the leader, and the servant *must* serve the Lord. The health of vertical relationships is entirely determined by how well the lesser succeeds at obeying, serving, and honoring the greater.

However, if our relationship with God is viewed strictly through the lens of vertical titles, then how we relate and interact with God will be based on obligated service. Just how a relationship with a boss is determined by how well you succeed at fulfilling her wishes, it can be very easy to let a similar top-bottom, hierarchical approach to relationship produce a works-based faith with God—the more you do for God determines his love and pleasure toward you.

But that is so deeply at odds with the love and grace God offers us through his Son, Jesus. That's why in John 15, Jesus introduces a new way to relate with God in a *horizontal relationship* where God is *with us.* He no longer calls us servants in a vertical relationship with him as our master, but instead, he calls us *friends.* We've been put on a level playing field with *Jesus Christ,* the Savior of the world, the Son of God himself. We don't have to *earn* anything, just as we don't have to earn the love of good friends. We just have to *be* with him.

How do we feel about that?

TENSIONS WITH BEFRIENDING THE LORD

Whenever I hear the concept of "being friends with Jesus," I can't help but think about the sensational music video "Jesus Is a Friend of Mine" by Sonseed. If you've never seen it, there are no words that do it justice. The image of the band says it all. In fact, if you have three minutes, just scan the QR-code here and take a listen. You won't regret it.

Did you watch it yet?

Did you?

Last chance.

It's seriously one of the most ridiculous music videos I've ever seen. *Hokey* is the best adjective I can think of to describe it. It's fun and cute and gets your head bobbing, especially during that wicked bass solo. You can't help but smile, and even let out a soft chuckle, when you listen to this song.

The band Sonseed • Jesus Is a Friend of Mine music video

But here's the problem: a lot of us may legitimately laugh at the idea of being friends with Jesus, just as we laugh at a ridiculously hokey music video that claims the same thing.

We feel tension with this! Even Jesus's disciples would have wrestled with the idea of moving from serving their Rabbi (and their *God*, for that matter) to being friends with him. We love knowing Jesus as our God, Lord, and Savior, who loves us and saves us from sin and gives us eternal life. We devote ourselves to serving him. We even go so far as to claim we have a "relationship" with him. Yet, for whatever reason, being friends with Jesus just doesn't seem . . . right.

I have a few hunches as to why we may feel tension about befriending the Lord.

1. ELEVATING SERVANTHOOD ABOVE FRIENDSHIP

Brian Edgar talks about how we almost think viewing Jesus as a friend is something reserved for immature Christians, those newer to their faith, or even a fun way for kids to understand their relationship with Jesus.[109] But it's not for us adults. Not us "veteran Christians," if we can even describe ourselves that way. It seems like at some point we should graduate in our faith from just hanging out with Jesus as a friend to doing as much as we can to serve him. It's just us trying to abide by God's commands, is it not? To be lesser? To be last? To serve? To pick up our cross and follow him? Local churches and preachers say the sign of spiritual maturity is how much we *do* for the Lord. Being friends with Jesus just seems like a downgrade when compared to being servants of Jesus. But again, this could be the result of us living out a works-based righteousness if we strictly view God through a vertical relationship without the addition of the horizontal relationship of friendship. Just as we can't make the mental leap of viewing our boss as a friend, it may be hard to do the same thing with God. Which leads to the second tension we have with befriending the Lord.

2. BEING INTIMIDATED BY GOD

Perhaps we prefer the vertical titles of God as King, Lord, and

Creator because of the distance between us and him. It helps us to see how much greater, holier, more successful, loving, and powerful he is than us, which is all certainly true. But are we guilty of using God's greatness as an excuse to exclude him from being intricately involved in our lives? Maybe we're afraid of befriending Jesus because so doing requires intimacy with a holy, all-powerful God. Perhaps we're showered with guilt from past hurts, bad habits, terrible decisions, and broken relationships that leaves us wondering, *How could a perfect God want to be friends with me? Doesn't he know who I am?*

We may say it's a wonderful dream and incredible ideal to be friends with Jesus, but it feels like it's impossible, just as it's impossible for us to befriend Steve Jobs, Taylor Swift, Beyonce, or Chris Pratt. So we view the likelihood of friendship with Jesus the same we do with a celebrity: unlikely and distanced, where we're painfully aware of our inadequacy in comparison to the elevated status and greatness of the individual. So in our inadequacy and shame, we keep him at arm's length.

But if that's our response, that may be more indicative of our past experiences with relationships than anything else.

3. REMEMBERING PAST FRIENDSHIP EXPERIENCES

This may be the greatest tension we have with befriending the Lord. At their best, friendships are a lot of fun. You could take those late-night Taco Bell runs together when you were in college, or go on adventure trips to the mountains together, or vent about life every once in a while. But as pleasant as friendships are, for many Americans, they're pretty surface-level at best. As we've already discussed, many Americans are hungering for a closer sense of intimacy with their friends. Surely a relationship with Jesus is far more than a fun, pleasant, surface-level friendship that involves liking comments and sending GIFs back and forth, right? Is that really all it boils down to?

And what about friendships when they're at their worst? Broken friendships can be *incredibly* damaging. Maybe you've been stabbed in the back far too many times by people you thought were your friends—who gossiped about you, lied to you, broke confidence, led you into destructive habits, or fell through on keeping promises. When we experience any form of trauma in this way, our brains will activate their defense mechanisms to prevent us from getting close to anyone out of fear that we're just going to be hurt again. If that's how we navigate close, intimate relationships, then it also directly influences how we approach a close, intimate relationship with God.[110]

If this describes the range of our experiences with friendship—from fun and pleasant at their best to incredibly damaging at their worst—why would we want our relationship with God to mimic that? Surely there is a better title than "friend."

But perhaps we struggle with being friends with Jesus because we do so from our world's broken version of friendship. What if our earthly experience of friendship isn't what Jesus had in mind when he called his disciples—and when he calls us—his friends? What if instead of letting our *earthly* friendships inform our friendship with Jesus, we let our friendship *with Jesus* inform our earthly friendships?

THE GRACE IN BEFRIENDING THE LORD

Here's the reality: Jesus calls us his friends. Period. Whenever we ignore his words in John 15 and default back to a vertical relationship strictly based on service, we're reinterpreting Jesus's words as "I do not call you friends, but servants." If that were true, then the gospel would be all about the Son of God coming to earth to turn his people into slaves, and works-based righteousness would be required to win your favor with God and earn your ticket into heaven. Such a misinterpretation of Jesus's intentions is detrimental to our faith. Brian Edgar says, "To think this way is to reverse the actual trend of Jesus' thought and to guarantee the development of a works-related and duty-oriented view of discipleship, rather than one permeated by the grace and love of friendship."[111] Solely viewing ourselves as servants to the King without also being friends of the King will yield a works-based faith that will suck the life out of us. It'd essentially be the equivalent to how well you do your assigned tasks given by your boss or following laws because it's your civil duty. That's how the Pharisees and teachers of the law approached their relationship with God. And Jesus vehemently disapproved of so much of what they did.

We need to take Jesus's words about being his friends seriously, because doing so can completely transform how we relate with God as well as take our current friendships to incredible new heights. This friendship with Jesus is a divine friendship. It is a bond founded on the greatest possible love that could exist between any individuals, and it is a love that transcends this world. It is a divine love that holds the three persons of the Holy Trinity together in perfect unity.

It is a love that lays down one's life for friends.

Jesus practiced this divine friendship through everything he did. God could've saved humanity in a ton of different ways. He could've just snapped his fingers and destroyed Satan and the power of sin once and for all, immediately setting free all our hearts to his will and fixing our problems. But he didn't. Instead, God saves us through an act of friendship that deeply resonated with how we're designed.

God sent Jesus to be *with us.*

To do life *with* us.

To befriend us.

Jesus's entire life was devoted to loving and serving and befriending every single type of person you could imagine because *he knew how we were designed.* We're designed for community. Therefore, it is no coincidence that God communed *with* us by becoming *like* us through the incarnation of his divine Son in human form.

However, Jesus's friendship with his creation climaxes when, out of his divine love for us, he literally lays his life down by taking our punishment and dying on the cross to save us from our sins. Doing so not only gives us the gift of true life on this earth and for eternity but also returns us to the same state of community with God and each other as it was at creation with Adam and Eve.

Jesus's life, death, and resurrection are the greatest acts of friendship in the history of humanity.

This is precisely why we need to view our relationship with God as a friendship, because friendship with Jesus is one entirely bound by *grace.*[112] Think about it for a second. Almost all of our vertical relationships are bound by some sort of obligation. A student *must* learn from his professor, an employee *must* work for her boss, and a child does not have the freedom to choose his or her biological parents. But friendship, on the other hand, is the only category of relationship that exists out of the freedom to choose to be in a relationship with another *solely for the sake of the person.* You are never forced to be in a friendship with someone—if you are, then it's not a friendship! There is no legal document, binding contract, or biological connection to tell you to remain friends. Rather, you're simply friends because you both freely choose to be. That's what makes friendships so powerful, because you did nothing to earn or deserve that friendship other than be yourself.

Tell me that is not the epitome of grace? Being friends with God, then, is the ability to live freely in his grace because you did nothing to earn his relationship or favor. Jesus died for you because he loves you. All we need to do is accept his friend request (pun intended). The twentieth-century German theologian Jürgen Moltmann says, "The concept 'friend' stresses freedom. Rightly understood, the friend is the person who 'loves in freedom.' This is why the concept of friendship is the best way of expressing the liberating relationship with God, and the fellowship of men and women in the spirit of freedom."[113]

Now here's the craziest part. Because we're designed for community, and science shows that we're shaped and formed by our most significant relationships, then being friends with Christ by communing with him through practices like prayer, solitude, scripture reading, worship, and gathering in Christian community, will form us more into his likeness. Befriending the Lord becomes the most transformative thing we could possibly do, because we are letting his friendship influence every aspect of who we are, just as God designed friendships to do. Brian Edgar puts it this way:

> This friendship [with Jesus], like all true friendships, is transformative. It is inevitable that friends become like those with whom they live closely and whom they appreciate, admire, and love. And so, as we live in friendship with Christ, we are transformed into his likeness. Friendship is the means by which believers are clothed with the new self and conformed to the image of Christ. Through friendship, we are made like our friend Jesus.[114]

When we take Jesus at his word—that we are no longer servants but friends—and we see God as a gracious God who gets on our level in a horizontal relationship, then the primary language for our relationship with God isn't just Lord-to-servant, King-to-civilian, or Master-to-apprentice. It is also friend-to-friend. Friendship moves from being the last term we'd ever use to describe our relationship with God to a primary term.

And this changes everything.

SERVICE REDEFINED

Jesus told us that the power that binds these spiritual friendships with each other is a mutually self-sacrificing love, right? "Greater love has no one than this: to lay down one's life for one's friends" (John 15:13 NIV). That means this friendship with Jesus is bound by emptying ourselves for the other, which is contrary to our individualism in not needing others. It's bound by sacrificing our desires for the other, contrary to our isolationism in not wanting others. This friendship instead is bound by a love that's based on serving.

Right after Jesus calls us his friends instead of his servants, he follows up in John 15:14 by saying, "You are my friends *if you do what I command*" (emphasis added). But that doesn't make any sense. Didn't Jesus just tell us that we're no longer servants? We're his friends, right? If we're not servants anymore, then why are we still told to serve him and follow his commands? Is this some bait-and-switch game Jesus is playing here?

While friendship with God still boils down to service, it's a different *kind* of service.

Jesus so heavily emphasized service during his three years of ministry with his disciples because he was ridding them of any power complexes and pride that may have existed in their minds to best prepare them to befriend Jesus. This is the Great Reversal of the Great Reversal, remember? As Edgar explains, according to the gospel, "Greatness is to be interpreted in light of servanthood, and servanthood is to be interpreted in light of friendship."[115]

We all know this to be true. Pride cannot exist in healthy friendships. In fact, selfishness is often the main reason why friendships get destroyed. That's why the best friendships are defined by mutual service to each other, not because they *have* to but because they *want* to. These kinds of friends are willing to do whatever is best for the other, so much so that they are willing to lay down their own desires because they love that other person so much. It's a mutual service done out of freely chosen love, not forced obligation.

The same is true for our friendship with Jesus.

While the role of service within our friendship with God doesn't change, what does change is the motivation behind our service. Edgar provides a table that compares the mind-set and motivation differences of a vertical servant-master view of God and a horizontal friend-friend view of God:[116]

Servant-Master Relationship	Friend-Friend Relationship
Does what the master wants	Does what the friend wants
Acts out of duty	Acts out of friendship
Obedience is the central virtue	Friendship and love are central virtues
Does not really know the master	Knows the friend intimately
A relationship defined by doing	A relationship defined by being
Servanthood is a requirement	Friendship is a gift of grace
Work oriented	Relationship oriented
Hierarchical in form (the lesser serves the greater)	Egalitarian in form (both parties serve each other equally)

Can you feel the difference between the two? Viewing our relationship with God as a friendship frees us from works-based righteousness, legalism, and the pressure to have our life together, and unleashes us to be fully loved by God and to fully love him in return.

We pursue him and his ways not because we *have* to but because we *want* to. Considering everything God does for us, how could we not do the same for him?

Furthermore, when we truly embrace God as a friend, we no longer have to hold him at arm's length, like a distanced celebrity. Rather, we can let him intimately know us, and we can intimately know him. His Holy Spirit is the perfect companion who literally goes with us everywhere we go, so we are never truly isolated. He is present in and helps us with everything we do, so we are never truly independent. When we can boldly live into that truth, then life in itself can feel a lot less lonely, because God is *always* there. We don't just have to devote fifteen minutes of our morning to reading Scripture or an hour on Sundays to worship. Rather, we can talk to him on our commute to and from work, or while we're getting groceries, or on a morning walk with our toddler. We can listen to worship music on our morning runs or read Scripture while we wait for the bus on our Bible apps instead of doomscrolling Facebook. We can serve others in our communities by replicating Jesus's example. Just as life is so much better when we can do it alongside our friends, it is infinitely more so when we're friends with Jesus. He becomes our constant companion who transforms how we navigate the entirety of our lives.

Most importantly, there is nothing we can do that will drive him away from us, unlike broken friendships from our past. The apostle Paul says in Romans 8:38–39,

> And I am convinced that nothing can ever separate us from God's love. Neither death nor life, neither angels nor demons, neither our fears for today nor our worries about tomorrow— not even the powers of hell can separate us from God's love. No power in the sky above or in the earth below—indeed, nothing

in all creation will ever be able to separate us from the love of
God that is revealed in Christ Jesus our Lord.

Nothing can separate you from God's love. That's what makes
Jesus the greatest friend we could ever have. He will never leave
you or forsake you. If this truth comes as a struggle for you, then I
suggest doing whatever you have to do to come to terms with Jesus's
love for you before moving forward. Spend time in prayer, journal
your thoughts, meet with a pastor, read through the Gospels, and
learn about the life and love of Jesus. Truly, there is so much freedom
and liberation that comes when we can declare with confidence that
"Jesus is a friend of mine."

———

If we want to be set free from our loneliness and experience true
relational satisfaction, it all starts with finding our security in the
freedom of God's grace through his friendship. This is so important,
because when we define friendship according to friendship *with
Jesus*, then this divine friendship becomes the template for how we
can go about our friendships with others here on earth. And when
our friendships are based upon the mutual pursuit of laying our lives
down to Jesus, the result is friendships that transcend what this
world has to offer, radically form us deeper into Christ's likeness,
and remedy our loneliness for good.

DISCUSSION QUESTIONS

1. Who's someone you've always dreamed of befriending? Why do
   you feel like you can't be friends with them?
2. How do you feel about being "friends with God"? How does that
   concept strike you?
3. Revisit the three tensions we may have with befriending the
   Lord: (1) elevating servanthood above friendship, (2) being intim-

idated by God, and (3) remembering past friendship experiences. Which of these three tensions do you resonate with the most? Are there any tensions you would add to this list?

4. How is your relationship with Jesus as a friendship going? How could it be more liberating?

5. What does cultivating a friendship with Jesus look like on a daily basis?

6. How could you let your friendship with Jesus influence how you go about your other friendships?

CHAPTER 6

FRIENDSHIP AS FORMATION

Bad company corrupts good character.

– 1 Corinthians 15:33 –

I have completed four Tough Mudder obstacle courses in my life-time. These races consist of jogging across ten miles of someone's donated farmland to complete a bunch of obstacles that aren't too different from summer camp team-building activities. Throw in a ton of mud and exclusively branded headbands, and you got yourself a Tough Mudder.

Despite how I fail to do about half of the obstacles and how sore I always feel (they serve as annual reminders that I'm indeed getting older), the sense of accomplishment that comes with finishing these races is comparable to none. But the best part is these races aren't designed for any single individual to accomplish on their own. In fact, some of the obstacles are impossible to complete by yourself. You *have* to rely on the people around you. Let me share some examples.

The Mud Mile 2.0 obstacle is a bunch of muddy humps with large pools of muddy water in between. The only way you can get over those humps is if someone is down in the pool giving you a boost, with someone on top of the hump lending you a hand to pull you up.

The Pyramid Scheme obstacle is a 120-degree ramp about thirty feet high. You're wet enough and it's steep enough that you would just slide down if you tried to run up it yourself. Instead, you need two people to form a base at the bottom of the ramp, with another person propped up on their shoulders, with yet another person propped up on *their* shoulders, acting as a ladder for others to climb up to the top.

Then there's Electroshock Therapy, an obstacle where you have to book it through thirty feet of dangling live wires that will shock you and knock you to the ground if you touch one. It's the worst. The only way you'll be motivated to do this obstacle is if you see others get through it first.

These are just three of the twenty-five obstacles. And after nearly four hours, my team and I completed it. The endorphins were surging. We felt like beasts. And we got free T-shirts.

The implications for the power of friendship behind this ridiculous (and overpriced) event are impeccable. Thousands of complete strangers rally together to help each other through obstacles. Fears are overcome, limits are pushed, new heights are accomplished, and memories are made. All this happens because everyone there is fighting for a common goal: to finish the race. (And get the free T-shirt.)

My 2019 Tough Mudder team

If that's not a perfect metaphor for the church, then I don't know what is. (Minus the free T-shirt. Except most churches give out free swag. So yes, including the T-shirt.) Overcoming our greatest obstacles becomes much more doable when we can do so alongside friends. They can take us to entirely new heights when we allow them. That's perhaps the most hidden power of our friendships: they can draw us closer to God himself while forming us into a better resemblance of his image. However, the inverse is also true—our friends can draw us *away* from God and reinforce our sinful ways. We are who we're with because our friends form us—both for good and for bad.

This doesn't just apply to our friends, of course; everything we do in our life is forming us into who we currently are and will be in the future. This is due to something we all experience as human beings whether we know Jesus or not—and it's called spiritual formation. So before we talk about how our friends form us for better or for worse, let me give you an overview of what spiritual formation is.

SPIRITUAL FORMATION: AN OVERVIEW

Why are you the way you are?

When we pause long enough to consider that question, we'll find that we are always in the process of becoming someone. There are a multitude of forces we are constantly exposed to that form us into who we are, what we think, and how we act. In his book *Practicing the Way*, John Mark Comer finds that we are formed by at least four basic forces:

1. The stories we believe. Much of who we are and what we do depends on the stories we believe. How do we view our bodies? What do we believe about God? How do we define what's good and evil? How did our family of origin distill in us our view of the world? What we believe determines how we act.

2. Our habits. "We become what we repeatedly do," Comer says. "The things we do, do something to us; they get into the core of our being and shape our loves and longings."[117] How we eat, what we watch, the social media algorithms we consume, and what we do when no one else is looking all form us into who we are.

3. Our relationships. We're already aware of this one, but just to drive it home again: *We are who we're with.* We are a gregarious species who morph and mold into the communities in which we immerse ourselves. A large portion of the stories we believe and our habits are reinforced by our relationships.

4. Our environment. All three of the above forces collide in our environment, which includes our nationality, ethnicity and racial group, state, city, workplace, socioeconomic status, and home life. These are the settings in which we do life and which form our cultural narratives.

After acknowledging these forces of formation, the question

remains: Do our stories, habits, relationships, and environments draw us closer to God's heart or away from God's heart? Our answer to this question matters, because it's not a matter of *if* we're being spiritually formed, but *how* we're being spiritually formed. Everything in our life is forming us either to be more like Jesus or to be less like Jesus. And if we're being formed to be *less* like Jesus, there are thankfully a number of things we can start doing instead that form us to be *more* like Jesus.

"Spiritual formation" is a long-lasting tradition in church history that dates all the way back to the early church fathers and monastics who were dissatisfied with how the world was influencing their lives. In a great act of defiance to the world, they got up, left their possessions behind, and retreated into deserted places to meet with God, learn his ways, and be *spiritually formed.* The ultimate goal in spiritual formation was to purge themselves of sinful habits by practicing the habits Jesus demonstrated, so they could grow "in union with God."

If you've grown up in the church or been in Christian circles for a while, you may have heard about practicing what's called the "spiritual disciplines." These are specific practices or habits we can do that *intentionally* form us into Christlikeness, as opposed to the unintentional habits that steer us away from Christlikeness each day. These disciplines include prayer, contemplation, Scripture reading, fasting, generosity, serving the poor, hospitality, sabbath, confession, worship, and many more. Perhaps you've even done some of these practices yourself!

But here's the kicker: rarely, if ever, is "friendship" considered a spiritual discipline. Despite our relationships being one of the most powerful formational forces in our lives, many Christians don't recognize friendship with others to be just as vital to their relationship with God as prayer, Scripture reading, and worship.

Thankfully, there are some monastics from church history who knew the power of friendship on our spiritual formation, and I want to introduce you to one of them: Saint Aelred of Rievaulx.

INTRODUCING ST. AELRED

Saint Aelred grew up in a highly educated and religious family in Hexham, Northumbria, located in northern England, in the early 1100s. At the age of fourteen or fifteen, Aelred was sent away to the court of King David I to continue his education. His studies required a familiarity with many classic texts, including the Roman philosopher Cicero and his treatise entitled *On Friendship*. Ever read a book that changed the way you view the world? Well, this particular work by Cicero had a considerable impact on Aelred that would go on to inform his theology of friendship (more on that in a moment).[118]

But after nine years of studying in the king's court, Aelred became discontent with his luxurious life and noble status. He believed there had to be something more to this life than riches and fame. So he did what many people did in that day when they wanted to experience a fuller life with God: abandoned everything he owned, left everyone he loved, and became a monk.

Aelred admitted himself as a monk just two days after visiting the Cistercian Monastery of Rievaulx in 1134, convinced it held the secrets to the deeper life he was longing for. After a decade of being a monk and practicing the monastery's way of life, Aelred was elected as the abbot (or leader) of Rievaulx in 1147. He held this position until his death twenty years later.[119]

As the abbot, Aelred was a spiritual leader to the monks at Rievaulx. He provided wisdom on prayer and living a disciplined life grounded in the love of God. He wrote several little books, called treatises, on a wide variety of spiritual topics. But one of his most substantial works was a treatise entitled *Spiritual Friendship*. This treatise, which is only 140 pages long, serves as a guidebook for cultivating healthy spiritual friendships with others. He discusses what virtues need to be practiced, which friendships ought to be avoided, how to practice discretion when befriending others, and more. Aelred asserts that when all these practices are properly observed, the result is deep friendships that intentionally form us into Christ's likeness and a relational satisfaction that is certainly capable of remedying feelings of loneliness. Aelred believed friendship "was a way in which [the love of God] could be experienced on earth" and "that the Christian faith could transform human friendship and raise it to new heights."[120] Aelred argues that true friendship mutually founded on the love of Jesus is the greatest good that can be experienced in this life, as it is a direct means to experiencing the love of God through a friend, with Christ gathered in their midst.[121]

As I discussed previously, psychology has shown us the quality of our friends largely determines our sense of self-worth, purpose, and quality of life. Then shouldn't it also be true that our friendships influence our spirituality as well? Our friends will either draw us toward holiness in God's image, or they will draw us away toward sin and self-seeking pleasure. The spiritual quality of our friendships matters in who we become and to our sense of well-being and belonging.

But before we can dive into the nitty-gritty of how to practice spiritual friendship, we need to identify the three different types of friends that form us, according to St. Aelred: carnal friendship, worldly friendship, and spiritual friendship.[122]

CARNAL FRIENDSHIP

The first time I looked at porn was because of a friend.

I was over at Jason's (not his real name) house one day when I was in the fourth grade. We were just playing with our action figures, as most fourth grade boys do, when Jason suggested, "Hey, we should look at naked girls on the internet." I didn't even know this was something I could do, so of course it piqued my interest. So we pulled up the browser on his family's desktop computer (since smartphones weren't a thing in 2004, we had to be extra cautious about it). After just a couple of minutes, I was enthralled.

A few weeks later, Jason was over at my house. After a few hours of hanging out, I suggested that we look up those images again. We weren't as cautious this time, though. Our babysitter caught us, told my parents, and I was grounded for two weeks. Little did I know as a fourth grader that my buddy had led me into sin. It was only a few years later I wound back up on the internet and developed a pornography addiction that haunted me through junior high school.

What took place with my buddy Jason is what Aelred would call a "carnal friendship," which he advises us to avoid at all costs.

The word *carnal* refers to "flesh," or literally, "meat." It includes the same root word that we see in *carnivore*, or meat eaters. In the New Testament, the Greek word *sarx*, which is translated to "carnal" or "flesh," is used to specifically refer to our sinful nature. Paul says in Romans 7:5, for example, "For when we were in the realm of *the flesh [sarx]*, the sinful passions aroused by the law were at work in us, so that we bore fruit for death" (NIV, emphasis added). So our flesh— our *carnality*—is our propensity to sin and disobey God's intentions for our life (read: to be *deformed*).

Therefore, carnal *friendships* are founded on sin. They "spring from mutual harmony in vice," as Aelred says.[123] They are lustful, sinful, and destructive, driven by selfish gain. There is no sense, reason, limitations, or wisdom that governs these friendships. Righteousness is the furthest thing from the mind, just as it was with me and Jason all those years ago. The irony about carnal friendships is that on the surface these friends consider themselves "blessed" because of how the bond makes them "feel." They still give each other a sense of belonging and acceptance. However, it is a false sense of blessedness, because the friendships are ultimately grounded in satisfying the passions of a wandering heart. When two enter a carnal friendship, it is formed out of a "sinful bond," which could lead to committing crimes, sacrilege, or other forms of sin on behalf of the other. Due to its foundation of sin, the friendship will eventually be "consumed by its own self," falling apart by the same means that formed the friendship in the beginning.[124] That's what sin does: it destroys and deforms. So it should be no surprise that a friendship founded on the destructive lure of sin is later destroyed by that same lure of sin.

A little later on in his treatise, Aelred says that you might be in a carnal friendship if it includes any of these five characteristics:

1. **Slander**—ruining the other's reputation
2. **Reproach**—bringing false accusations and lies against the friend
3. **Pride**—refusing to admit one's faults and heal the friendship
4. **Divulgation**—revealing one's secrets that were told in confidence
5. **Persecution**—dissolving the friendship through acts of hatred

Aelred doesn't provide any concrete examples of what a carnal friendship looks like, but such a bond could include prostitution, illicit sex, abuse, gang activity, bullying together, scams, toxic work environments, judgment, tribalism, and so on. Or, if anything, these are friendships that in the end just don't make you feel that great about yourself.

Another way to describe carnal friendships in modern terms is what psychologist Henry Cloud labels as "bad connections." These are relationships that impart on the other perfectionism, lofty expectations, unreasonable demands, critical spirits, shame, guilt, and put-downs, which produce feelings of fear, guilt, and inferiority. Such relationships ultimately lead to the deconstruction of ourselves, which implies that growth simply cannot happen in such relational conditions.

Now, I know what you're thinking: *Why would anyone even want to be in a carnal friendship if they're so destructive?* Well, remember: the human brain is *wired* for connection, so much so that it would rather be in abusive, destructive, and sinful connections with others than to have no connections at all. This is what the relational neuroscience suggests.[125] Although carnal friendships may create a sense of belonging, they aren't founded on the mutual love of Christ and thus do not produce character, virtue, or growth into the image of God.[126] Aelred strongly discourages any friendship that would be "unbecoming of the good" and should therefore be avoided at all costs.[127] He knew the formational power our friends have on us. He echoes the same sentiment when Paul says in 1 Corinthians 15:33 that "bad company corrupts good character," or when Proverbs 22:24–25 says, "Don't befriend angry people or associate with hot-tempered people, or you will learn to be like them and endanger your soul." This is why Aelred warns us not to befriend these types of people, as they would cause detrimental damage to our faith and uprightness.[128]

Put simply, while carnal friendships can relieve our loneliness, they do not benefit our souls. And the draw toward carnal friendships can be particularly tempting among young adults. As I mentioned earlier, as young people we can lose our sense of self when we submit to a tribe to which we wish to belong. When moving to college, we may get swept up into the sex and drinking culture or other negative habits simply because it's what everyone else is doing, even if they were raised to avoid such habits. The stories I hear from students in my context support this trend. Students come to college and commit sinful acts with carnal friends, not necessarily because they want to *sin* but because they don't want to be *alone*. Sometimes, it's tempting to think it's better to sin with our friends than to be holy by ourselves. To reiterate Henry Cloud's statement, the brain prefers any connections—even bad ones—over no connections at all.

WORLDLY FRIENDSHIP

Aelred's second category of friendship is what he calls "worldly friendships." The thing about worldly friendships is that there isn't anything evil about them, especially to the degree of carnal friendships. But there's also nothing inherently virtuous about them either. Ultimately, Aelred says these friendships are formed for personal advantage. If carnal friends are founded on sin, worldly friends are founded on the self. To put it simply, worldly friends just want to have a good time so they can feel good.

Say you develop a friendship with someone because you found some things you have in common. This excites you, so you proceed to exchange contact information, hang out, and spend time together. You grab coffee, you study together, you laugh and have a good time. You bond over your favorite sports team or working out. You laugh at the same memes you text each other. You share the same opinions about politics and how this country should be run. As far as you know, things are great. What could possibly go wrong?

Well, that's the thing. What *could* go wrong is exactly what would cause a worldly friendship to end. The strength of our friendships is revealed when our lives get tough. But since a worldly friendship is based on the selfish gain of how you make each other feel, there isn't a selfless motivation to help you when you encounter a difficult situation. Perhaps they don't want to insert themselves into your "mess" or even work through a sharp disagreement that arose between you. In these moments, the friendship just got *hard*. Now it costs you something. In that moment, the selfish motives behind the friendship are revealed. The "friend" was never fully in it for you. They were in it for how it made them feel.

This is why Aelred says these worldly friendships can be filled with deceit, intrigue, and selfishness, while lacking certainty, constancy, and security. As soon as the personal benefit of the friendship is gone, then so will they be gone. "Take away his hope of profit, and immediately he will cease to be a friend," Aelred says.[129] These friendships may exhibit a unique combination of sinful and virtuous tendencies that are unbeknownst to us, since their ultimate goal is personal satisfaction instead of pursuing God's will.[130] This makes worldly friendships a "fork-in-the-road" type of friendship, bearing the potential to become either a spiritual or a carnal friendship.[131]

Although Aelred has little more to say on worldly friendship, I would argue this category defines most of contemporary friendships. The Greek philosopher Aristotle similarly categorized this bond as "pleasure friends," where two people pursue the pleasure of friendship to make each other *feel good*, rather than pursue the virtue of friendship to *make each other good*.[132] Since the Enlightenment, friendship has turned from a public good that betters society to a private good that benefits us as individuals.[133] Essentially, worldly friendships align with our individualistic and consumeristic approaches to friendship. As I discussed in chapter 3, everything should meet our precise expectations in a consumer culture. If the product ceases to be useful to us, it can be returned or forgotten. Worldly friendships function from a similar motive: people become products to benefit ourselves, and the friendship can be left and ghosted once it ceases to be useful.

The pursuit of virtue, humility, and God's will is not the foundation for worldly friendship. The focus is how the friendship makes the other person feel, how it eradicates one's loneliness or fills an inner emptiness, without the desire to reciprocate those actions to the other. While worldly friendships certainly can boost our mood, remedy loneliness, and grant us purpose, they are only temporary in nature, as they cannot fully remedy our deep-seated need for committed community according to God's design. Further, as Aelred says, a friendship that ends wasn't a friendship at all.

However, there is a fine line between a healthy reliance on our hardwiring for human connection and utilizing others to satisfy personal needs. Friendships can become idols when they are used to heal what only Jesus Christ can heal. As Kelly Needham notes in her book *Friendish*, friendships can be a means to God, but they must not become gods in themselves.[134] Thus, the trust, transparency, and humility required for the deep friendships we need to flourish can best be found in the enduring commitment of Aelred's third category: spiritual friendship.

SPIRITUAL FRIENDSHIP

Spiritual friendship is the highest quality of friendship someone can have with another. Rather than being founded upon sin or self-seeking pleasure, this friendship is founded upon Christ himself. Aelred obviously has a lot to say about spiritual friendships (it is the title of his treatise, after all). So let's break down his thoughts.

1. SPIRITUAL FRIENDSHIP STARTS WITH CHRIST'S LOVE FOR US

First, we have to have a firm grasp on Christ's own love for us before we can begin to love each other as Christ loves us. This is why learning how to befriend the Lord, as we talked about in chapter 5, is so important. Our friendship with Jesus serves as the template for how we cultivate spiritual friendships. Aelred's take on friendship is largely influenced by 1 John 4:15–16: "Whoever confesses that Jesus is the Son of God, God abides in him, and he in God. So we have come to know and to believe the love that God has for us. God is love, and whoever abides in love abides in God, and God abides in him" (ESV).

The language of "abiding in God" and "God abiding in us" illustrates how two friends can bask in each other's presence through their selfless love for one another. You can't be friends with someone if you don't love them. Thus, the truest form of friendship is based upon God's love. Therefore, if God is love, and his version of love is the foundation for true friendship, then Aelred radically concludes that *God is friendship*.[135] If we want to know the fullest possibilities of what our earthly friendships can be, we have to start with the foundation of our friendship with God by regularly abiding in the grace he gives.

2. LOVE EACH OTHER AS CHRIST LOVES US

When we come to terms with how much God loves us and the extent Jesus went for us, then we have a better idea for how we can replicate Christ's love for us to our friends. Jesus said it himself: "Love each other *as I have loved you*" (John 15:12 NIV, emphasis added). First John 3:16 similarly states that "this is how we know what love is: Jesus Christ laid down his life for us. And we ought to lay down our lives for our brothers and sisters" (NIV). We need to love each other as Christ loves us.

Of course, this could look like laying aside our selfish desires and serving our friends in times of need (or at the very least letting them choose what pizza we're ordering for game night). That's a mark of a good friendship. However, Christ's sacrifice wasn't just laying aside a selfish desire to help us overcome some problem in our life. His sacrifice literally unlocked a new capacity for us to relate with God and overcome our sins through the power of the Holy Spirit living in us. Therefore, if we are to love our friends as Christ loved us, then the best way we can lay down our lives for our friends is to help each other relate with God and overcome our sins *together* through the power of the Spirit. Laying down our lives to help each other pursue Jesus is the greatest act of service we can do for our friends. When we do so, we radically grow in our friendship with each other *and* God. The ultimate aim of spiritual friendship, above all else, is to help each other better know God, discern his will, and walk in obedience.[136] And when we do so, we are able to recognize Christ's very own presence gathered with us.

3. CHRIST'S PRESENCE IN OUR MIDST

Aelred says that when we gather with our spiritual friends, the very presence of Christ is there too. At the very beginning of his book, when one of Aelred's friends sits down beside him, he writes, "Ah, here we are, you and I, and I hope a third, Christ, is in our midst."[137] This is a reference to when Jesus says in Matthew 18:20, "For where two or three gather in my name, there am I with them"

(NIV). To Aelred, true friendship is being together *in Christ*. He's right there with us.

What would happen to the dynamic of your conversations over coffee if you acknowledged Christ is sitting there too? Or how would your morning run with your buddies change if you realized Christ is running with you? Acknowledging Jesus's presence in our midst can completely change the dynamic of our friendships. My friends who ran the Tough Mudder with me served as a constant reminder that I wasn't doing this alone, and pushed me to greater heights because of it. In a similar way, acknowledging Jesus's real presence when we're with our friends serves as that constant reminder that we're not alone in our faith, and we can push each other to greater heights because of it. This is why Aelred says that through Christ our friendships are not merely a matter of flesh and blood, because our *spirits* are involved. We bond at the soul level.

4. FRIENDSHIP IS DISCIPLESHIP

If we recognize Christ's very presence when we gather with our friends, that he is the force drawing us and binding us together, it changes how we interact with each other. If the pinnacle result of Christ laying his life down for his friends is so we may grow in communion with God, then the purpose of doing the same for our friends is so we may see *them* grow in communion with God and his church. At that point, friendship is no longer just a pleasant entity that benefits our personal desires, as most Americans perceive it. It's far greater than that. According to St. Aelred, spiritual friendship *is* discipleship. The word *disciple* simply means "student," "learner," or "apprentice." In the context of Scripture, discipleship refers to the full orientation toward and adoption of Jesus's teachings and lifestyle into our own way of life. So if the greatest way we serve our spiritual friends is helping one another grow in their faith and orient their lives to the way of Jesus, then we are, in essence, practicing discipleship.

A lot of churches may frame discipleship as a weekly program their congregants attend or as a veteran Christian helping a newer Christian navigate their faith. And those are great things. But truly, one of the most powerful ways we can be discipled into the life of Jesus is praying with our friends whenever we want. Or studying Scripture with our friends without a formal program facilitating it. Or attending Sunday worship services together, or doing ministry together, or intently listening to one another confess their sins, worries, or fears. *All* of these activities are means to utilizing the power of the Holy Spirit to bind us together and form us into Christ's likeness. Friendship of this spiritual caliber not only satisfies one's relational needs, but it also draws friends into deeper intimacy with the Triune God—together.[138]

5. BECOMING CHRISTLIKE

Remember: we are designed for community. The people we spend the most time with mold our brains and shape our central nervous systems, which determine our feelings, decisions, values, and more.[139] Our friends literally form our psyches.[140] Which means they also form our souls. Simply put: if we are who we're with, then we become Christlike when we're with Christlike friends. When we spend the most time with our spiritual friends, then God will use them to mold us into his image and form us into people of virtue. Author Brian Edgar sums up this point perfectly when he says, "Virtue cannot be achieved in solitude. Friendship, specifically virtuous friendship, is at the heart of Christian community. One needs friends in order to be holy."[141]

Spiritual friendship is not based on feelings or self-gratification but on serving and bettering each other. It is not a means to pleasure, but its end is pleasurable in itself because it is selfless and good. Since friendship is discipleship, spiritual friends share common morals, pursue similar life interests, guard their passions, fight for justice, and strive toward growth in benevolence as we chase God's heart together.[142] These bonds become a laboratory to practice and receive the transformative love of Christ. Such an approach to friendship flies in the face of worldly and carnal friendships. Brian Edgar says, "The whole point of friendship in the monastic tradition is that it is not satisfied with the average; it seeks nothing but the best in the other, and that means the greatest possible faith and love."[143]

In contrast to the five vices of carnal friendship, Aelred lists the following four virtues as core components to spiritual friendships when they're founded upon the mutual pursuit of Jesus:

1. **Love**—Enacting upon the good for the friend
2. **Affection**—Expressing how the other makes you feel
3. **Security**—Serving as a safe haven for each other
4. **Happiness**—Celebrating in all things together

6. THE MEDICINE OF LIFE

This is why Aelred says spiritual friendship is one of the greatest goods we can experience on this earth. There truly are no other friends quite like those who go all in on their love of Jesus together. That's why these friendships can elevate our joy during good times, ease our pain during hard times, rebuke us in times of correction, and overall function as the "medicine of life."[144] Just like how morphine can greatly reduce our pain, spiritual friendships make the hardships and suffering of this life so much more bearable.

I've heard it said that true friendship "doubles our joys and halves our sorrows." Spiritual friends are there for you when life gets tough, unlike worldly friendships. *Nothing* can separate you from their love because their love is based upon the same inseparable love of God (Romans 8:38–39). These friends are a safe place to confess hard feelings, entrust secrets to one another, and offer correction without causing each other pain. They help you bear your burdens and refuse to run away when they encounter your mess, unlike worldly and carnal friendships. These types of raw, vulnerable experiences naturally grow us closer to one another. But it also means *all* of life's joys can be celebrated with spiritual friends. Yoga class, book clubs, playing Super Smash Bros., playdates with your kids, going to parades, enjoying a bonfire, and celebrating a promotion all become infinitely more enjoyable when can we do them together with these friends.

That's not to say you can't enjoy these things with nonspiritual friends. But because of the unique spiritual quality that the mutual pursuit of Jesus brings to them, spiritual friendships are capable of providing a deep satisfaction that other friendships can't quite replicate. And that could be because eternity is stamped on these friendships.

7. SPIRITUAL FRIENDSHIPS ARE ETERNAL

Finally, Aelred says that when all our spiritual friendships are lived out to their maximum potential, spiritual friendships are a visible sign of God's coming kingdom. It is through Christ-rooted friendships that we get a taste of the unity, the charity, the goodness, and the love that will be found in eternity when Jesus returns to restore his creation.

That's why I believe spiritual friendships can literally be considered our BFFs—our best friends forever. Why? Because spiritual friendships are truly the best, and they literally last forever. These friendships have *eternity* attached to them, because we are all saved in Jesus. No relationship gets better than that! If we think spiritual friendships make this life on earth that much more tolerable and enjoyable, how much better will it be when we reunite with God at the end of all things together, when there will be no more tears, suffering, and death? When God restores heaven and earth, we will fully reclaim our God-given design for community when Jesus resurrects us and brings us together to live in perfect union with God and each other as spiritual friends—just the way he intended Adam and Eve to live at the very beginning.

———

My friends take me places I never thought I'd go. They push me to accomplish Tough Mudder races. They spot me in the gym to strengthen my chest presses. They get me to try new foods, embark on new experiences, and do things I could never do on my own. I am a far better person because of my friends. They have formed me.

And that is particularly true with my walk in Jesus.

I am a better follower of Jesus because of my spiritual friends. On every second Monday of the month, Paul, Nate, and I help each other process our fears, stressors, and joys, all with Christ gathered in our midst over breakfast. Mason calls me out of my sin and challenges me in areas I am otherwise blind to. In our small group that meets on Tuesdays, we share our highs and lows of the week, discuss content from a book, and pray for one another's struggles at the end. And my wife, Kasey, my dearest spiritual friend, certainly doubles my life's joys and halves my life's sorrows. She has seen me cry more than any other person, and she reminds me daily of God's love for me.

Spiritual friendships are truly the greatest good we can experience on this earth, aside from Christ himself. They produce a relational satisfaction that meets our needs, strengthens us, remedies our loneliness, and all around makes this life so much more worth living—not just for now but for eternity.

So how do we actually develop these friendships? How can we distinguish the carnal, worldly, and spiritual friends in our life? And how do we know which friends to prioritize who will maximize our formation into Christlikeness, minimize our deformation into sin, and remedy our loneliness for good?

That's where the Friend Zone Matrix comes in.

DISCUSSION QUESTIONS

1. What was a time when friends helped you do something that you could never have done on your own?
2. Do you have any friends (either past or present) that you'd classify as carnal friends? What is or was it about those friendships that leads you to classify them as such?
3. Do you have any friends (either past or present) that you'd classify as worldly friends? What is or was it about those friendships that leads you to classify them as such?
4. Do you have any friends (either past or present) that you'd classify as spiritual friends? What is or was it about those friendships that leads you to classify them as such?

CHAPTER 7

WHOM YOU SHOULD BEFRIEND

The righteous choose their friends carefully,
but the way of the wicked leads them astray.

– Proverbs 12:26 (NIV) –

I made a terrible first impression on Damian.

I had just moved to Sioux Falls, South Dakota, to start my two-year pastoral apprenticeship at The Ransom Church. The other resident pastors and I were invited to join some young adults from our church for a Labor Day weekend hangout. We grilled out, played yard games, and had a grand ole time. This gathering was particularly crucial for me, because, quite frankly, I had no friends in Sioux

Falls yet. So a lot was at stake for me to begin finding community in my new city.

As I've already alluded to, I'm a very, *very* extroverted person. I'm also a very energetic person. But when you place my extroverted, energetic self in a room of people I'm desperate to befriend, I could come across as a little . . . exuberant. Obnoxious even.

After we ate our hot dogs and finished playing corn hole (or "bags," according to South Dakotans), about four or five of us went back to the apartment to cool down. Damian was one of them. As we were gathered in our friend's living room, I broke the silence.

"Hey guys, have you ever heard of anti-jokes?" I asked. Everyone shook their heads. "Well, you're about to find out. What's green and has four wheels?"

"A tractor," one of them says.

"Nope. Grass! I lied about the wheels." Everyone muttered a pity laugh, and I queued up the next one. "What's brown and sticky?"

"Uh, poop?"

"Nope. A stick!" They smiled and rolled their eyes. But I kept going. "What's yellow and can't swim? . . . A school bus!"

Nothing.

"Why'd the koala fall out of the tree? . . . Because it died!"

Nada.

"What's red and bad for your teeth? . . . A brick!"

Silence.

"What's worse than a bee sting? . . . Two bee stings!"

So here I was, spewing out anti-joke after anti-joke, thinking they were the funniest things in the world (my sense of humor is truly unmatched). But years later, one of my now best friends, Damian, told me how completely oblivious I was to the fact that *everyone* wanted me to stop telling anti-jokes after the second or third one.

This was *especially* the case for Damian. *Who does this guy think he is?* he asked himself. I later came to find out that I left such a bad first impression on Damian that he was resolved not to befriend me.

But again, I was *desperate* for friendship. Perhaps that desperation became apparent by trying a little too hard to make a good impression through anti-jokes (admittedly, there are way better ways to make a good first impression). Although Damian was totally put off by me at this first meeting, I thought he seemed like a pretty cool dude. He was highly involved at The Ransom Church, loved Jesus, and overall seemed like a loveable guy. So I put myself out there and asked him if we could grab dinner sometime, having *no* idea about the bad impression I had apparently left on him.

Thankfully, Damian accepted my invitation.

We grabbed some Vietnamese cuisine for dinner and coffee afterward, and our friendship has only taken off from there. I officiated Damian's wedding, and he served as our kids ministry director at the church we planted. Damian has dedicated my kids to the Lord during Sunday services, and our families go on annual vacations together.

All this to say, my friendship with Damian may never have happened if I hadn't chosen to pursue it further. There was a discernment process about whom I would befriend as a lonely young adult in a new city. I didn't just ask myself, *Whom do I want to be friends with?* I had to choose the *right people* to befriend who would intentionally form me into Christlikeness.

THE FRIEND ZONE MATRIX

As we've discussed so far, we are spiritually formed by our friends. If we are who we're with, then we need to be cognizant of the *spiritual quality* of our friends and their impact on our discipleship to Jesus. Aelred warned us of the dangers of carnal friends, as they are built upon a mutual desire to pursue vice and sin. These friends ultimately turn us away from God. Worldly friends, although pleasant and pleasurable, are surface level at best. You may have a lot in common and make each other feel good, but they may bail on you as soon as conflict arises or the friendship gets messy. This is why spiritual friendships that are mutually founded on the pursuit of Jesus are the greatest good we experience on this earth. It's in these friendships we can give and receive the love of God.

However, while Aelred discusses the varying spiritual qualities of our friendships, he doesn't talk about the varying *depths* of friendship we can have with other people. We may have best friends, close friends, distant relatives, acquaintances, peers, mentors, coworkers, bosses, spouses, and more. Dunbar's number and the four circles of friendship prove this to be the case. We can't be best friends with all these people, and not everyone bears the same influence on our formation as others do. Even Jesus in his humanity didn't have the same depth of friendship with everyone! So how can we identify the varying depths of our friendships and assess their impact on our formation, relational satisfaction, and loneliness?

Well, to do that, I want to introduce you to a tool I've developed called the Friend Zone Matrix. It all began after I was literally put in the dreaded "friend zone" by a girl I had asked to be my girlfriend back in 2017. I was so upset. I couldn't help but feel like "just being friends" was such a downgrade from being boyfriend and girlfriend. While I was drowning in the flood of my misery, though, I made this realization: Why is being in the "friend zone" with anybody a bad thing? Shouldn't it be a good thing? What if there are a variety of "friend zones" we can be in with others? So out of a moment of rejection and heartbreak (okay, I wasn't that sad about it, but I was still pretty bummed), I pieced two-and-two together from these early days of my research on spiritual friendship, loneliness, and belonging, and the Friend Zone Matrix was born.

The Friend Zone Matrix has two axes. The X-axis plots the *depth* of your friendships and is based off a concept called the Four Spaces of Belonging that Joseph Myers explains in his book *The Search to Belong*.[145] The Y-axis, on the other hand, plots the *spiritual quality* of your friendships, according to Aelred's carnal, worldly, and spiritual categories. Lastly, the gradient illustrates the *impact* the friendship has on your formation through three colors: red for the damage of carnal friendships, yellow for the middle ground of worldly friendships, and green for the growth of spiritual friendships. The gradual fade in intensity from left to right demonstrates the increase in the friendship's influence on our formation the closer those friends are to us, according to relational neuroscience.[146] (If you want to see the Friend Zone Matrix in full color, visit YouNeed-Friends.com/resources.) Put it all together, and it looks like this:

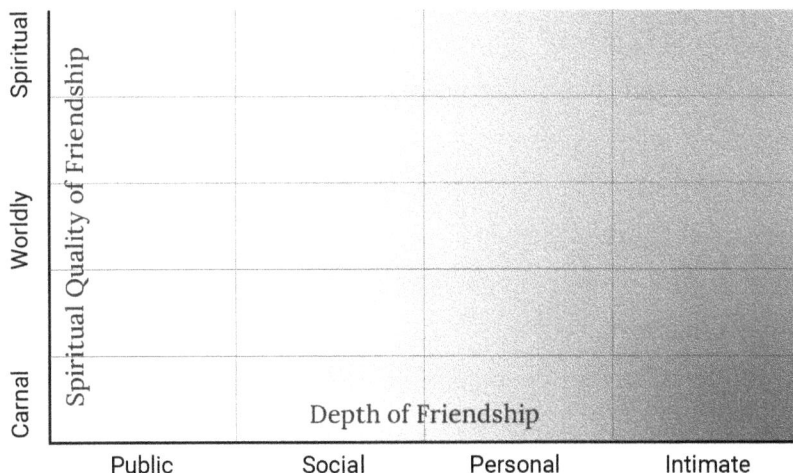

The Friend Zone Matrix

So here's how we'll break down the Friend Zone Matrix. First, I'll summarize each of the Four Spaces of Belonging according to

Myers's work. As I describe each space, I will demonstrate how Jesus himself related with others in that space, and how Aelred's three spiritual qualities of friendship can apply to our friends in that particular space. After I've described all of the Friend Zones, then I will show how you can plot your relationships on the matrix to get a sense of your belonging and spiritual formation from your friends—and what you can do about them if they're not where you'd like them to be.

Ready? Let's dive in to the first set of friend zones.

THE PUBLIC FRIEND ZONE

The first of the Four Spaces of Belonging on the left side of the X-axis is called the public space. This space consists of a large group of people who gather together for a common purpose. Although no one knows each other in the public space, everyone gathered is connected through a similar outside influence. Take a sports game, for example. Thousands of strangers pack a stadium and bond over the common purpose of rooting on their team toward victory. Or take when you go to the grocery store. Despite being surrounded by total strangers, you're still gathered in that public space for the same purpose: buying groceries. Attending church can be considered a public space, because you are gathered with others for the same purpose of worshipping God, despite not knowing everyone in the same room.

Jesus related with people in the public space all the time. We see him constantly immersed in crowds, such as synagogues, city streets, or a countryside when he fed five thousand people. All of these people were gathered to hear Jesus teach and experience his miracles. Now, although Jesus in his divinity knew every single person intimately (he is the Son of God), Jesus in his humanity still related with them as strangers with whom he interacted maybe once during his earthly ministry.

Public spaces are environments in which we immerse ourselves every day while sharing them with others. The vast majority of public spaces are morally neutral: grocery stores, coffee shops, student centers, high schools, malls, restaurants, bowling alleys, offices, and gyms. If we were to use Aelred's terms, these public spaces would be considered "worldly" spaces solely because they benefit us. They aren't "evil," drawing us away from our formation with God, per se, but they also aren't necessarily drawing us toward God either. Therefore, these places we regularly visit—and the friends we might encounter there—could be plotted in the Public-Worldly Zone on the matrix.

However, as it relates to our spiritual formation and sense of belonging, the key aspect to determine about the public spaces we regularly inhabit is whether they are *carnal* spaces or *spiritual* spaces.

A place in the Public-Carnal Zone is one that will draw you toward sin. Examples include bars that may pressure you to drinking more alcohol than you want, brothels where prostitution takes place, a toxic workplace where employees take advantage of clients, or casinos that encourage gambling and greed. Although you may not know anyone personally in these carnal spaces, the fact that sin and living contrary to God's ways are common practices there will inevitably deform you the more time you spend there.

On the other hand, a place or crowd in the Public-Spiritual Zone is one that will draw you *toward* God and holy living. Church is the prime example. Being surrounded by other Jesus followers in worship and hearing a sermon are clearly better for your spiritual formation than a brothel or casino! But other gatherings in the Public-Spiritual Zone could include midweek ministries at church,

Christian camps and conferences, public prayer meetings, monas-teries, para-church community centers, worship concerts, or any event that gathers believers together. These are way more likely to influence your formation in a positive way and open the door for you to meet new spiritual friends.

Now, let me clarify: I'm not saying you should abandon *all* the public spaces you go to and *only* attend Christian concerts, Christian schools, Christian coffee shops, Christian grocery stores, Christian gyms, or Christian restaurants (although only ever eating at Chick-fil-A does sound like heaven on earth). The key is to avoid spending excessive time in any places or crowds in the Public-Carnal Zone that will draw you toward deformation, instead opting for spaces in the Public-Spiritual Zone.

THE SOCIAL FRIEND ZONE

The second space of belonging is the social space. Myers says this space consists of between sixteen to thirty-two "entry-level" friendships that are mainly defined by small talk. This would be the equivalent of the thirty-five people in the third circle of friendships according to Dunbar's number. These people share "snapshots" of who they are, casting small glimpses of themselves that let you determine if you wish to develop a closer relationship with them. These relationships have short, spontaneous interactions and nor-mally do not dive too deeply into personal matters. Social relation-ships could be neighbors, coworkers, a barista, mutual friends of your spouse, a serving team at church, members of a small group, or good friends you enjoy spending time with but who don't know you all that well.

So when I gathered with that new group of people for the Labor Day party all those years ago, we had entered each other's social space. We didn't pour out the deepest parts of ourselves to each other, but we did share *just enough* to get an idea of who everyone was. This is where we started seeing each other's personalities, discovering common interests or hobbies, and feeling out the potential of becoming friends. It was here in the social space that I got the snapshot of Damian as a pretty cool guy, which is why I extended the invitation to get to know him more. (But it was also here in the social space that Damian got a snapshot of me as an obnoxious teller of anti-jokes!)

Jesus in his humanity interacted with people in the social space all the time. One example, seen in Luke 10:1–20, is when he sent out seventy-two of his disciples into the mission field. We commonly hear about Jesus's twelve disciples, but we rarely hear about his *seventy-two* disciples. This was a larger group he interacted with but not to the depth we see with his core group of twelve disciples. Jesus would also spend time with larger groups of people in their homes, such as when Matthew invited Jesus and his disciples over to his home as dinner guests "along with many tax collectors and other disreputable sinners" (Matthew 9:10). Similar to any large social gathering we may have, this would have been a perfect space for these tax collectors and sinners to share snapshots of themselves to Jesus and his disciples, and vice versa.

Now, it's here in the social space that we can start to get an idea of whether these people may be carnal, worldly, or spiritual fiends. You may observe that a Social-Carnal friend has some particularly sinful habits, whether that's coarse joking, vulgar language, negative outlooks on certain people, toxic work habits, and so forth. Whatever it is, you can get an idea that these people have a higher propensity toward a more deformative lifestyle that could impact your own spiritual formation if you were to get closer to them in the personal or intimate spaces.

A Social-Worldly friend may be someone who's fun to be around, with whom you have good banter and share several common interests that make a good entry-level friendship. However, you haven't fully gotten to know them deeply enough to discover whether they are going to draw you toward or away from Jesus. This is a middle-of-the-road, feel-good friendship that could go either way.

Lastly, a Social-Spiritual friend is someone you can clearly see has similar Christian values. Sometimes you can pick this up just by how people carry themselves. Truly committed disciples of Jesus just have a different way of living their day-to-day lives than other people. Some snapshots they might share of themselves may include mentioning their faith in brief conversation with you, having stickers from their church on their water bottle, or even attending the same church and small group as you. These snapshots are important, as they indicate the potential spiritual qualities that can really press you forward into your spiritual formation and sense of belonging.

THE PERSONAL FRIEND ZONE

The personal space consists of four to sixteen closer friendships where you can disclose a fuller picture of who you are. This would also include the fifteen friends in your close- to best-friend inner circles according to Dunbar's number. These are the friends who *get you.* You feel more at home with them. You don't have to maintain a certain image of yourself like you do with those in the social space (such as the small talk you have with the Great Clips employee cutting your hair). Together you spend time at these friends' homes, bring your kids to playdates, participate in small groups, embark on road trips, go out to dinner, and help each other with house projects. Any activities that foster more meaningful connection are usually done with friends in the personal space. But again, most importantly, you are free to be *yourself* with these friends. You can move beyond sharing "snapshots" of yourself and be more open and vulnerable about the personal aspects of your life without feeling uncomfortable or worrying that you're oversharing, all while knowing your friends won't be repulsed by what you share. They maintain confidences.

Jesus's friends in the personal space would have been his twelve disciples. Jesus spent a lot of time with a lot of people, but his twelve disciples were with him the most. They went *everywhere* with him. Being a disciple of a rabbi required them to go where he went, eat what he ate, and even sleep where he slept. They did ministry together, laughed together, traveled together, suffered together, and did life together.

Now, here's the kicker with the Personal Friend Zones. Because we spend more time with these friends, they are the ones who start to have a larger impact on our formation. This is when we need to be particularly keen on where our personal friends fall on the carnal, worldly, or spiritual spectrum. Our relational neuroscience expert, Amy Banks, asserts it's tempting to pick our one or two highest-quality friendships as the ones who have the largest impact on our behavior, even if we don't stay in consistent contact with them.[147] But remember: the people we spend the most time with shape and form our brains the most. So it's here in the personal space when their spiritual qualities become the most apparent and therefore the most determinative of our own formation and sense of belonging.

Friends in the Personal-Carnal Zone love to sin together. Maybe they wouldn't come right out and say that "sinning" is their favorite recreational activity, but that is what undergirds these friendships' actions and motivations. The mutual pursuit of Jesus is far from the minds of Personal-Carnal friends. In fact, participating in sinful activities may even be considered *fun*. Excessive partying, crude humor, debauchery, sexual immorality, greed, and distorted outlooks on life are central to these relationships. However, while you don't have to hide your true self from them, you may tend to hide this true version of yourself around *others* to mask the sinful habits you have with these friends. At that point, you begin to live a double life that isn't authentic with everyone you meet. Who you are with others in the public and social spaces isn't congruent with who you *really* are and what you *really* do with these Personal-Carnal friends.

Additionally, you may have a great time with Personal-Carnal friends, and you may feel fully known, but deep down, you may wish you could break out of the habits that these friendships have introduced into your life. However, you continue in these carnal friendships because they're better than the alternative of being isolated and alone.

Now, friends in the Personal-Worldly Zone are also a blast. You gain so much pleasure from these friends. You also feel like yourself around them, where you can talk about anything and enjoy each other's company. Chances are good that personal-worldly friends aren't *as* steeped in sin as personal-carnal friends. But you still sense something is lacking. These friendships are fun, yes, and you can open up more about your life, true. But these friendships may still leave you wondering, *Is this all my friendships have to offer?* They may not be forming you into a person deeply steeped in sinful habits, but they also aren't forming you into a better follower of Jesus. They may make you feel good *as* a person, but are they making you *into* a good person?

This is where Personal-Spiritual friends really shine. These are good friends who share a common love of Jesus with you, all while pursuing the things of God in their own individual lives. You may study Scripture, pray, attend church services, and attend small groups together with personal-spiritual friends. But the key difference is that you are spending more of your life together. You move beyond the weekly rhythms and parameters of church attendance and small group gatherings and spend extra time together that is unplanned, unhurried, and organic. It's spending time around a bonfire where you can talk about a struggle you're going through, or having your friends and their kids over for dinner just to talk about life and pray together before parting for bedtimes, or having all your friends over to celebrate a huge life accomplishment.

The irony with friends in the Personal-Spiritual Zone is that they don't seem as spiritual at first glance, because you're not always doing something explicitly "spiritual," like praying or reading Scripture or attending church services. But what is just as, if not more, spiritual is being more fully known and present with others who are mutually chasing Jesus. The way you live out your friendship with Jesus *together*, even while doing fun activities that seem to have no spiritual significance whatsoever, like a riveting game of Spikeball, shapes and molds and forms your soul in greater ways than you can imagine. Further, these friends help you live more fully into who Christ has called you to be, causing you to feel more aligned with your true sense of self, and therefore lessening the temptation of leading a double life around people in the public and social spaces.

THE INTIMATE FRIEND ZONE

The last but certainly not least zone is the Intimate Friend Zone. This zone of friends only consists of one to three people, but these few people know the deepest parts of you without judging, shaming, or ridiculing you. These are the few close and intimate friends of Dunbar's inner circle, such as a spouse, romantic partner, family member, mentor, or best friends. The level of trust in these friendships is much higher than any other friendship due to the sensitive information that is shared. You are fully known in these friendships. You literally have nothing to hide.

Jesus's intimate friends were Peter, James, and John. These three disciples saw more of Jesus's life than any other disciple. For example, six days after Jesus revealed himself as the Messiah, he took Peter, James, and John up a mountain to be alone with God. What happens next would have *floored* Jesus's three intimate friends, as they saw Jesus's appearance transformed with a shining bright white light, revealing his divine glory (Matthew 17:1–8). That's certainly a powerful example of Jesus revealing the full extent of himself to his three best friends that no one else got to witness. But perhaps an even more powerful example was when Jesus took all twelve of his disciples to the garden of Gethsemane on the night he would be betrayed and handed over to be crucified. When they arrived at the garden, he left the eight other disciples behind and took Peter, James, and John deeper into the garden where he became "anguished and distressed" (Matthew 26:37). He turned to his three closest, dearest friends and said, "My soul is crushed with grief to the point of death. Stay here and keep watch *with* me" (Matthew 26:38, emphasis added).

In Jesus's most vulnerable moment, he invited his three closest friends to be there with him. He was free to express his grief, anguish, and distress to them that no other disciple witnessed. He had nothing to hide.

It's debatable if you could even have an Intimate-Carnal friend where you share the deepest parts of yourselves with another person who is steeped in sin. Intimate friends are people who know things about you no one else knows, but sin's destructive power would still be embedded in the bedrock of the relationship. Some possible examples of Intimate-Carnal friends are partners having sex outside marriage, best friends taking drugs together, or even abuse occurring between spouses. Nonetheless, these friends are participating in degrading activities that are detrimental to their formation in Jesus. Unfortunately, because these relationships are so intimate, they are much harder to break off, and they bear exponentially more influence over your livelihood, well-being, and relationship with Jesus than less intimate friendships.

Obviously, friends in the Intimate-Worldly Zone are a step in the right direction. You can still share the deepest part of yourselves without getting caught up in sinful and destructive habits characteristic of Intimate-Carnal friends. In fact, Intimate-Worldly friends can still be very beneficial for you and your formation, especially if it means you are confessing things about your life that no one else knows about. There is so much freedom that comes with confession and being fully known (which we will discuss at length in chapter 9). The only caveat is that worldly friends still bear the risk of leaving the friendship if things get too difficult. You may be there for this friend through difficult seasons in his life, but he gets squirmy and uncomfortable when he needs to reciprocate similar support when *your* life gets hard. But even in the best-case scenario where your Intimate-Worldly friends are fully supportive and can be completely candid with you, there is one thing they are missing that will bring the depth of their friendship to the next level: a mutual friendship with Jesus.

Friends in the intimate space can be fully vulnerable with each other about the deepest, darkest parts of their lives without any fear of judgment or ridicule. But the difference with friends in the Intimate-Spiritual Friend Zone is they can do so with *God* by their side. The shared pursuit of Jesus adds a layer of depth to spiritual friendships because they more accurately reflect the type of community God designed us to have. To revisit the creation narrative, Adam was not fully human until God created Eve to live in communion with one another *and God*. A core part of the perfection of Adam and Eve's communion was precisely because they could be naked and unashamed (Genesis 2:25). This literally refers to their physical nakedness, but it also refers to how they could fully know and be fully known by each other and God, with nothing to withhold from one another.

When I was doing my doctoral research, interviewees identified two elements that constituted deep friendships: first, that they can openly share about deeply personal matters, as I discussed in chapter 3, and second, that they have a common faith in God. Our faith is a lofty topic that is highly personal, as it deals with questions pertaining to what is good and the meaning of life, the study of Scripture, prayer, and other practices that engage our souls. When we can be vulnerable about our lives while pursuing the love of God with our friends, we simultaneously grow in our union with God *and* one another. This is precisely why Aelred calls spiritual friendship the greatest good we can experience on this earth.

PUTTING IT ALL TOGETHER

Now that we have a firm grasp of all the Friend Zones, we can now begin plotting our friends on the Friend Zone Matrix to get a bird's-eye view of the formational power of our current friendships and our overall sense of belonging. From there, we can come up with a game plan for what to do next. Let's look at some examples of how someone can utilize this tool.

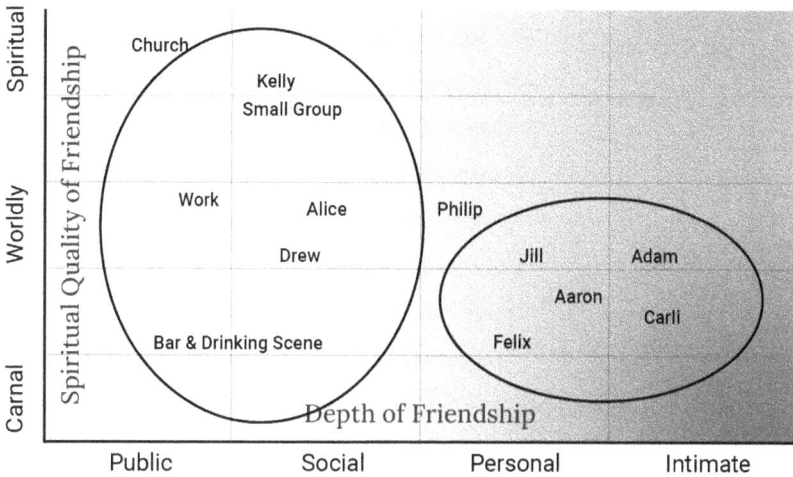

Figure 1: Steve's Friend Zone Matrix

According to Figure 1, Steve attends church and is part of a small group, which are positive environments that can form him spiritually and teach him about the Bible. He also has been getting to know a new Christian friend at college named Kelly who sits by him in a business class every Monday, Wednesday, and Friday. However, Steve is also involved in the bar and drinking scene, leading him to compromise in certain areas of sin. Although he attends church and a small group, his closest group of friends, whom he spends the most time with, are not actively pursuing Christ's way of life. He has found that Aaron, Carli, and Felix, in particular, lead lives that influence him away from fully living into Christlikeness as he's been learning about at church recently. Despite being involved in church and a small group, as well as becoming acquaintances with Kelly in the social space, relational neuroscience suggests Steve's worldly and carnal friends are more influential over his formation since they are in the personal and intimate spaces of belonging.

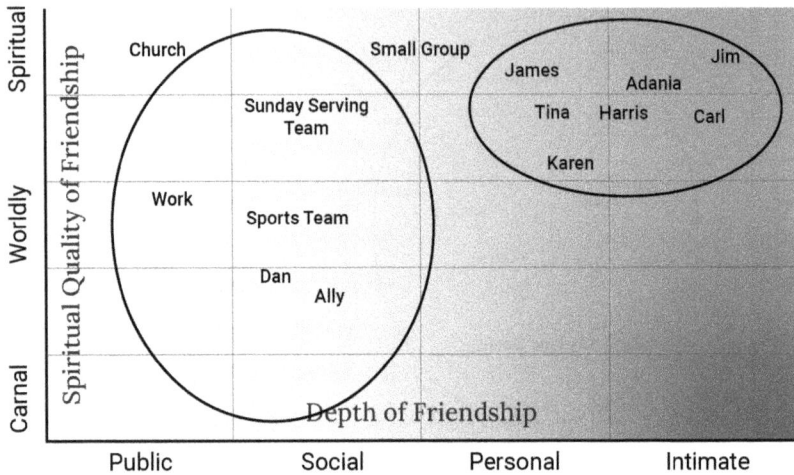

Figure 2: Sherry's Friend Zone Matrix

Now take a look at Sherry's example in Figure 2. Sherry also attends church and is part of a small group. However, she has plotted the small group closer to the personal space since they have been meeting together for almost two years now, which suggests she has a closer bond to her small group than Steve has. She works a secular job and is involved on a sports team, which is an encouraging outlet for her but also includes some individuals who don't lead as spiritually formative lives. However, her closest friends in the personal and intimate zones display St. Aelred's qualities of spiritual friendship. They regularly spend time together, love Jesus, attend church, and are safe spaces to talk about their deepest struggles. She even put Jim, her fiancé, in the top right Intimate-Spiritual Zone. Although she is still involved with some worldly and even carnal friends, Sherry is more likely to be formed spiritually because she is consistently around spiritual friends as her home base. In fact, since she belongs to a close-knit community founded upon the mutual love of God, she is better able to minister to those in her worldly and carnal friend zones without being influenced by their ways of life, since they are only in the public and social spaces.

SO DOES THIS MEAN WE CAN'T BE FRIENDS WITH NON-CHRISTIANS?

Now, I know what you might be thinking by now. If we are spiritually formed the most by Personal- and Intimate-Spiritual friends, does that mean we just shouldn't be friends with non-Christians?

No. We absolutely *should* be friends with non-Christians..

First, it's a little presumptuous to assume non-Christians are inherently deformational. There is a big difference between worldly and carnal friends. There are so many amazing, good, and kind people in this world who don't know Jesus who will lay their lives down for you as your friend. In those instances, they may actually be a great witness to the love of God written in their hearts, even if they don't know Jesus personally. The biggest difference, though, is they won't form you into greater knowledge of God and his holiness simply because they are not pursuing God themselves. You would need to find other friends who are if you want to be spiritually formed.

Second, it's important to note that Aelred makes the distinction that although we are not meant to be close friends with everyone, since carnal friends can be unbecoming to our good, we are still called to *love* everyone. Aelred does not discourage ministry to those with carnal tendencies. Jesus himself was a "friend of . . . sinners" (Matthew 11:19), yet his friendship with such people was grounded on the basis of loving service rather than mutual vice, as in the case of Personal- and Intimate-Carnal friends. The friendships between Christ and sinners would not be considered "spiritual friendships" by Aelred's standards because they are not mutually pursuing holiness on each other's behalf.[148] Aelred does advise, though, that if a carnal person's life exhibits other positive traits, then you can have entry-level interactions with him in the social space in the hope that he may be healed from those vices and later be admitted into a deeper friendship. Aelred even gives the example of Jesus befriending Matthew, a sinful tax collector, who gradually grew through Christ's influence and later joined Christ's tight circle of personal friends, the twelve disciples.[149]

Ultimately, having a strong foundation of Personal- and Intimate-Spiritual friends is necessary for our spiritual formation and sense of belonging, and so that we may be better able to minister to a carnal or worldy friend who doesn't yet know Jesus. In fact, as a Social-Carnal friend grows in her discipleship to Jesus, then she may begin moving up into the Personal-Spiritual Zone as time goes on.

Lastly, just because your spiritual friends have a mutual pursuit of Jesus also doesn't mean that they'll be "sinless." Although these friendships are not primarily founded on sinful desires and activities, we are all still carnal beings with temptations to wander from the heart of God. Although we may be chasing Jesus, we will still fall short in our righteous living, and we will inevitably hurt each other, say something insensitive, or cause drama. Therefore, it is just as crucial that any sins committed against our friends are quickly acknowledged, confessed, and repented of, in order to reconcile the friendship, regardless of their spiritual quality.

―――――

As Proverbs 12:26 says, "The righteous choose their friends carefully, but the way of the wicked leads them astray" (NIV). Whom we befriend matters. Our deepest sense of belonging comes from living fully into the friendship Jesus has to offer. Cultivating a spiritual friendship with God himself heals us of our pain and grants us freedom to be fully known and loved. One of the greatest forces that can form us more into Christlikeness, though, is our friends. By utilizing the Friend Zone Matrix, we can identify our sense of belonging with our current friends, the impact they have on our spiritual formation, and identify next steps to grow friendships closer and deeper.

But here's the unfortunate truth: over half of Americans feel like they don't have personal and intimate friends. In chapter 1, I mentioned how loneliness isn't just physical isolation or having zero friends. People can feel lonely even if they don't have deep enough friendships with people they can confide in with their deepest struggles. For over half of Americans, their Friend Zone Matrix may look something like this:

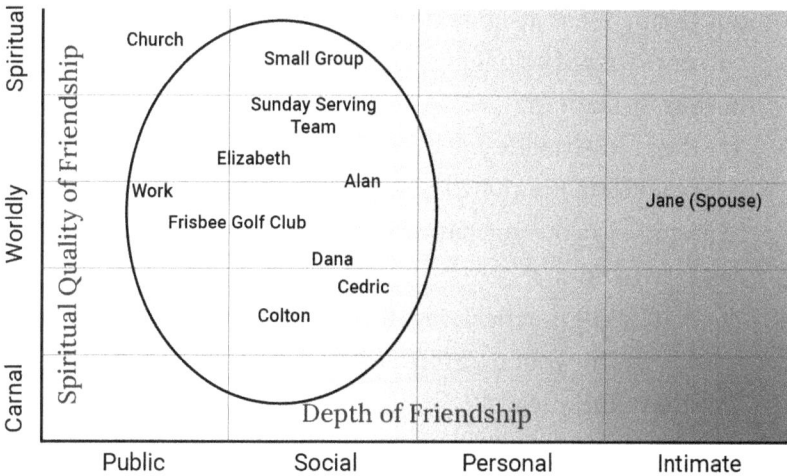

Figure 3: Caleb's Friend Zone Matrix

Other than Caleb's wife, he doesn't have *any* personal or intimate friends whom he can share deeper parts of his life with. And that *will* impact his sense of belonging, feelings of loneliness, and his formation into Christlikeness. Loneliness doesn't just ensue when you don't have any friends whatsoever or live an isolated lifestyle. Loneliness also occurs when you have friends who don't fully know you.

If the loneliness epidemic is to be remedied, it involves us befriending others at these deeper spiritual levels where they can be fully seen, known, and loved, as well as share in a mutual pursuit of Jesus. And in order to do that, we need to start with getting acquainted with the brothers and sisters we didn't even know we had.

DISCUSSION QUESTIONS

1. Think of when you decided to invest more time into a friendship. What was it about that person or situation that inspired you to do so?

2. Look at the blank Friend Zone Matrix on page 141. If you were to start plotting your friends on the matrix, where would you put them? What insights does the matrix give you about your current sense of belonging and the role your friends are playing in your formation?

3. Are there any friends you would like to get closer to who would help your formation? Are there any friends you need to pull back from to help your formation? What are some next steps you can take to do so?

4. What are some practical ways for you to invest in closer spiritual friendships for your own formation while still investing in those who don't know Jesus?

CHAPTER 8

THE BROTHERS AND SISTERS YOU DIDN'T KNOW YOU HAD

There are "friends" who destroy each other,
but a real friend sticks closer than a brother.

– Proverbs 18:24 –

There's no relationship I have that can quite compare with the one I have with my brother, Andrew. Not only are we bound to each other by our family's bloodline, but we know each other in ways that no one else does. We can each recall embarrassing stories about the other from our childhood and memories made on family vacations. We spent countless nights staying up late playing Halo 3, Super

Smash Bros., and Call of Duty: Nazi Zombies, while eating a heinous amount of Papa John's Pizza and Cheez-It Crisps. There are inside jokes and references we still crack today that date all the way back to when we were in high school that no one else understands. When Andrew finished his best man speech for my wedding by saying, "I've seen these two cats meow, and it's about to be a fancy feast tonight," I was the only one who knew that he was quoting Games Dean from *Video Game High School*, our favorite show back in 2012.

No one else knows me like the guy I literally grew up with. That's why our siblings, if we have them, can be some of the best friends we ever have. They experience all of life with us, even when we were our most awkward, pubescent selves in junior high. There is an intimacy inherent to sibling relationships. That's why I love how Proverbs 18:24 defines a real friend as someone who sticks closer than a brother or sister.

Perhaps you think that friendships of that level are rare and too hard to come by. It turns out, you have access to a multitude of brothers and sisters you didn't even know you had who bear tremendous potential in reclaiming your design for community and remedying your loneliness for good. In fact, every Christ follower has them.

They are found at your local church.

And yet, far too many Christians live like they're an only child in God's family.

THE DECLINE OF FAITH AND RELIGION

It's been made abundantly clear that we are designed for community. We flourish when we are connected with others, and we suffer when our loneliness goes unchecked. We are meant to be in an intimate friendship with our God *and* fellow believers. But what's unfortunate is many Americans—even Christians—don't have any personal or intimate friends who truly know them. This is due in large part to the various cultural forces like individualism and isolationism that are driving us deeper into lonely lifestyles. But they may also be driving us out of Christianity and the community of the church *altogether*.

Perhaps it's no coincidence that the loneliness epidemic has increased while religious affiliation and church attendance has decreased.[150] A study done by the Pew Research Center found that 65 percent of Americans identified as Christian in 2019—a twelve-point decrease from a similar poll conducted ten years prior—and those who are religiously unaffiliated increased from 17 percent in 2009 to 26 percent in 2019.[151]

These stats are significant considering the important role community plays within religious institutions. For two thousand years, people found their sense of belonging and community through church, whose gatherings serve as a unique time to find encouraging friendships while growing in the Lord together. Simply attending religious services and singing songs together boosts our sense of community and belonging, in addition to the twice as frequent face-to-face interactions practicing Christians spend together compared to non-practicing Christians![152] Having a group of people who share common beliefs on life, spirituality, and the world is a significant piece to finding belonging. But if people are walking away from the church every year, it raises the question of whether they are replacing the community of the church with other friendships that share a close commitment to pursuing virtue together (assuming they felt a sense of community in the church to begin with).

Although Americans' religious affiliations are declining, their sense of spirituality is not, fascinatingly enough. It's common practice today for someone to consider himself "spiritual but not religious" (or SBNR, for short). Being SBNR takes America's infatuation with individualism and consumerism and applies it to their spirituality. It becomes a privatized journey to achieving one's elected identity and elastic morality according to his own personalized standards, objectives, and convictions, all without the community of a religious institution telling him how he ought to live his life. Thomas Parkinson says, "The privatization of faith and the corresponding decline in faith communities are happening alongside an overall loss of community in America. . . . In a culture that so highly values individualism, many are living out their own private journey, completely separate from others."[153]

More and more people are placing their faith in the religion of individualism, where the god we worship is *ourselves.*

This has significant implications for Gen Z and young adults in particular, as we are the least religiously affiliated generation to date.[154] In 2018, Barna found that 42 percent of Gen Zers identified as Christian, 17 percent as Catholic, 7 percent as other faith, 8 percent as agnostic, 13 percent as atheist, and 14 percent as "none of these." One in three Gen Zers—35 percent—do not belong to a religion.[155] This is due in large part to being the first generation raised in America's post-Christian society.[156] Our lack of religious affiliation is due not only to our personal choices but also to being raised by more religiously unaffiliated parents than any prior generation.[157] Therefore, our starting point to faith and spirituality is truly post-Christian.[158] Instead of letting God's Word be the foundation of a good life, it's our sense of self—individualism. Jean Twenge notes, "In a society where young people hear 'If it feels good, do it' and 'Believe in yourself,' religion seems almost countercultural."[159] And with Gen Z being the most diverse generation in history, the thought of being a part of a religion that excludes people of other faiths or is judgmental toward people's lifestyle choices is a major turn-off.[160] If we are free to define our own morality to match our identities, then we will likely avoid external sources of moral authority as guiding principles for our life—like organized religion or church.

With this worldview, it becomes easy to adopt a "pick-and-choose" type of religion where we can embrace the parts of Christianity that make us feel good and avoid everything else that challenges how we want to live. As Tim Elmore notes, Gen Z values pragmatism over principles.[161] Our source of morality is not based on objective values that transcend humanity, but whatever it takes to advance our lives forward. In their comprehensive study of Gen Z, Barna notes:

> Their lack of confidence [in objective truth] is on pace with the broader culture's all-out embrace of relativism. More than half of all Americans, both teens and adults, agree with the statement 'Many religions can lead to eternal life; there is no one true religion. When that kind of universalism is paired with deep confusion about the nature of truth, it's impossible to assess the 'truth' of one's beliefs.[162]

Individualism is the new religion for many in the United States. But what's unfortunate is this form of spiritual individualism has also finagled its way into the Western church and our approach to Christianity.

LONELY CHRISTIANS ARE CONTRADICTIONS

If Christians function under a similar individualistic worldview, then our religion also becomes a spiritual means to self-development. Some Christians might ascribe to a set of orthodox Christian beliefs, try to be a good person by their own efforts, and attend church every once in a while when they aren't embarking on a kayak-camping adventure over a weekend. In fact, they might even say they don't need to go to church *at all*. They could just watch a worship service online, read Scripture silently, pray in private, fast, and do every spiritual discipline by themselves, and then attend a one-hour service whenever it's convenient for them.

These people might label this way of life as great spirituality. But it is *awful* Christianity.

A lonely, isolated Christian is a contradiction in terms. It was never Jesus's intentions that one of his followers could attend a church service without even being known by other believers, let alone navigate life's hardships by themselves. That is a pseudo Christianity inspired more by American individualism and isolationism than Christ's convictions. John Mark Comer says, "But we simply are not meant to follow Jesus alone. The radical individualism of Western culture is not only a mental health crisis and growing social catastrophe; it's a death blow to any kind of serious formation into Christlike love. Because it's in relationship that we are formed and forged."[163]

Following Jesus isn't a path toward self-help, nor is church a service for us to consume. So it raises the question, How could involvement in Christianity and its worshipping communities provide us with a greater sense of community and friendship that we may be longing for?

As it turns out, receiving salvation from our Friend Jesus doesn't just mean we're saved from our sins; it means we are adopted into a *family* through whom we can be fully seen, known, and loved.

It's time for a family reunion with the siblings we didn't know we had.

WHEN THE CHURCH WAS A FAMILY

As we discussed in chapter 3, the majority of the world was, and continues to be, a collectivist culture where individuals ascribe to a way of life that benefits the prevailing group to which they belong. And that primary group was their *families*. This was the dominant worldview of ancient Mediterranean culture, and it undergirded Jesus's life and ministry during his time on earth. Jesus said and did a lot of things that called out culture and flipped it on its head. But one thing he did *not* critique was his highly relational, family-oriented culture.

Joseph Hellerman writes extensively about this in his masterful work *When the Church Was a Family*. Hellerman identifies three main characteristics that made up the collectivist society in which the early church was founded and were assumed would be carried into future iterations of the church—including our Western individualist culture.[164]

1. A "GROUP COMES FIRST" MENTALITY

Whereas America is considered a "weak-group society," ancient Mediterranean culture was considered a "strong-group society." People valued allegiance to the group over meeting their individual needs *for the sake of the group's survival*. Your personal decisions entirely revolved around what was best for the group to survive and thrive. This culture was not nearly as resourced as we are in the United States—a reality we often take for granted. People in the Ancient Near East simply could not chase their own individual dreams, because they had to make sure the well-being of their group was taken care of first and foremost. This leads to Hellerman's next characteristic of collectivist cultures, that family is everything.

2. FAMILY IS EVERYTHING

The most important group you could have belonged to in that day was your family. That's why you see throughout Scripture chapters upon chapters of genealogies that we couldn't care less about. We barely know who our great-grandparents are, let alone who our great-great-great-great-great-great-great-great-grandparents are. Read 1 Chronicles chapters 1 through 8. I'm not kidding.

Everything you did was for your family. Your family decided what you did for a living, where your primary residence was, and even who you married, because it was all about ensuring your family survived and thrived for generations to come.

This was particularly why collectivists arranged marriages. In our culture, we marry someone for relational satisfaction, often based on commonalities we have, what we enjoy about one another, and if we can see a future together. But in collectivist cultures, marriages were arranged for their children to create strategic alliances with other families to increase their social standing, which simultaneously furthered their chances of survival.

This is a really important distinction to make. When we think of family, the priority is placed on the horizontal relationship to our spouse on the family tree, and then our kids second. We think the marriage relationship between husband and wife should be the most important and intimate relationship. But in collectivist, patriarchal families, the priority is not placed horizontally between spouses but vertically on the father's bloodline. Hence the chapters upon chapters of Scripture remembering great-great-great-great-great-great grandfathers. Therefore, husbands and wives would have held stronger allegiance to their father's bloodlines than they did to each other. Spouses were simply the intersection of two patriarchal bloodlines.

But here's what's particularly startling about Jesus's collectivist culture. Due to the commitment to the vertical relationship of the father's bloodline, the closest relationship someone could have in New Testament culture was not the bond between a husband

and wife but the bond between siblings. And that leads to the third, and perhaps most startling, characteristic of collectivist cultures involving siblings.

3. YOUR SIBLINGS WERE YOUR BEST FRIENDS

This was because siblings belonged to the same bloodline, whereas the husband and wife belonged to different bloodlines. Again, the commitment was stronger vertically on the family tree. But what's even more mind boggling to us is that sibling bonds took priority over marriage bonds. In fact, the emotional intimacy and support we often consider to be characteristic of good marriage relationships today were more so demonstrated in sibling relationships in the New Testament collectivist culture! That's why stories of sibling rivalries and betrayal in the Old Testament captivated these people so much, because sibling rivalry was the greatest form of betrayal someone could commit in a collectivist culture.

This was the culture in which the church was founded. The group came first. Your family was everything. And your siblings were your best friends. But that was then. Why should this matter so much to us today? The reason this matters so much to us is because salvation wasn't just about being saved from your sins and receiving Jesus as your personal savior. Salvation was about joining God's *family*.[165]

JOINING GOD'S FAMILY

When Jesus was recruiting his disciples, they weren't just choosing to follow an individual. They knew that his invitation into discipleship was to *join his group*. So although they left their families to follow Jesus—a huge deal in a strong group culture—in so doing, they joined a *new* family. In Matthew 19, Peter reminds Jesus of this:

"We have left *everything* to follow you! What then will there be for us?"

Jesus said to them, "Truly I tell you, at the renewal of all things, when the Son of Man sits on his glorious throne, you who have followed me will also sit on twelve thrones, judging the twelve tribes of Israel. And *everyone who has left houses or brothers or sisters or father or mother or wife or children* or fields for my sake will receive a hundred times as much and will inherit eternal life. But many who are first will be last, and many who are last will be first." (Matthew 19:27–30 NIV, emphasis added)

Do you see that? There is an implication that when you follow Jesus, your primary family is no longer your immediate family but *God's* family.

Another instance when Jesus claims his followers are family occurs in Mark 3. Jesus and his disciples are ministering to a large group of people gathered in a house near Jesus's hometown. In typical Jesus fashion, he's teaching truth that simultaneously amazes his hearers and frustrates the religious teachers who were also gathered there. His immediate family caught wind of this, and they traveled to this house to round Jesus up and get him out of there. They were concerned Jesus was causing a ruckus with the teachers of the law due to his controversial teaching (per usual), but they also wanted to protect their family's reputation from said ruckus. Here's how the scene unfolds when his family arrives:

Then Jesus's mother and brothers came to see him. They stood outside and sent word for him to come out and talk with them. There was a crowd sitting around Jesus, and someone said, "Your mother and your brothers are outside asking for you."

Jesus replied, "Who is my mother? Who are my brothers?"

Then he looked at those around him and said, "Look, these are my mother and brothers. Anyone who does God's will is my brother and sister and mother." (Mark 3:31–35)

The original readers of Mark's Gospel would have been shocked by this story. Remember, family is *everything* in a collectivist culture, so much so that the word *life* was often used interchangeably with the word *family*. So if one's family is synonymous with one's life, then rejecting his family was synonymous to losing his life. What Jesus does in this passage is he *denies* the authority of his immediate family, which equates with denying his own life. But in so doing, Jesus defines who his true family is: "Anyone who does God's will" is Jesus's brother and sister and mother. This, in turn, makes those who do God's will siblings to *one another*. Spiritual brothers and sisters.

Let's look at one more example when Jesus gives these difficult words in Luke 14:25–27:

> Large crowds were traveling with Jesus, and turning to them he said: "If anyone comes to me and does not hate father and mother, wife and children, brothers and sisters—yes, even their own life—such a person cannot be my disciple. And whoever does not carry their cross and follow me cannot be my disciple. (NIV, emphasis added)

This was such radical advice to a collectivist culture! Granted, Jesus isn't *literally* saying you should hate your family to follow him. In fact, Jesus teaches on the importance of loving your immediate family in other parts of the Gospels. But what he's getting at in this passage is when you follow Jesus, you don't just receive his salvation. You also join his family. Jesus's call to follow him and be his disciples assumed you wouldn't just follow him for your own personal benefit but that you would join his group of surrogate siblings.

Joseph Hellerman poignantly says,

> To follow Jesus meant to join Jesus' community. The thought that one could somehow acquire a "personal relationship with

God" outside the faith family—and remain an "unchurched Christian"—was simply inconceivable to those whose lives had been defined from birth by the groups to which they belonged. To become a Christian was to change groups, plain and simple.[166]

In essence, the early church approached their relationships with one another as an uncompromising, undivided loyalty to one another that was the equivalent of sibling loyalty then and the equivalent of spousal commitment today. Hence, we get Jesus's command in John 15:12–13: "My command is this: Love each other as I have loved you. Greater love has no one than this: to lay down one's life for one's friends" (NIV).

Metaphorically, Christ's disciples were spiritual siblings, but literally, they were friends. This implied that their friendships with one another were to function as if they were loyal siblings. That's why early Christians preferred to call each other "brothers and sisters" because their sibling language better communicated the deep commitment they had to one another. Get this: The word *Christian* appears only two times in the New Testament. But the Greek word *adelphos*, meaning "brothers and sisters," appears 316 *times*, and it is almost always used in reference to followers of Jesus. Here are just seventeen examples of the 316:

1. Romans 1:13: I want you to know, **dear brothers and sisters**, that I planned many times to visit you, but I was prevented until now.
2. 1 Corinthians 1:10: I appeal to you, **dear brothers and sisters**, by the authority of our Lord Jesus Christ, to live in harmony with each other.
3. 2 Corinthians 1:8: We think you ought to know, **dear brothers and sisters**, about the trouble we went through in the province of Asia.
4. Galatians 1:11: **Dear brothers and sisters**, I want you to understand that the gospel message I preach is not based on mere human reasoning.

5. Ephesians 6:23: Peace be with you, **dear brothers and sisters**, and may God the Father and the Lord Jesus Christ give you love with faithfulness.

6. Philippians 1:12: And I want you to know, **my dear brothers and sisters**, that everything that has happened to me here has helped to spread the Good News.

7. Colossians 1:2: We are writing to God's holy people in the city of Colosse, who are faithful **brothers and sisters** in Christ.

8. 1 Thessalonians 1:4: We know, **dear brothers and sisters**, that God loves you and has chosen you to be his own people.

9. 2 Thessalonians 1:3: **Dear brothers and sisters**, we can't help but thank God for you, because your faith is flourishing and your love for one another is growing.

10. 1 Timothy 4:6: If you explain these things to **the brothers and sisters**, Timothy, you will be a worthy servant of Christ Jesus, one who is nourished by the message of faith and the good teaching you have followed.

11. 2 Timothy 4:21: Do your best to get here before winter. Eubulus sends you greetings, and so do Pudens, Linus, Claudia, and **all the brothers and sisters**.

12. Philemon 1:7: Your love has given me much joy and comfort, **my brother**, for your kindness has often refreshed the hearts of God's people

13. Hebrews 3:1: And so, **dear brothers and sisters** who belong to God and are partners with those called to heaven, think carefully about this Jesus whom we declare to be God's messenger and High Priest.

14. James 1:2: **Dear brothers and sisters**, when troubles come your way, consider it an opportunity for great joy.

15. 2 Peter 1:10: So, **dear brothers and sisters**, work hard to prove that you really are among those God has called and chosen.

16. 1 John 3:10 So now we can tell who are children of God and who are children of the devil. Anyone who does not live righteously

and does not love other believers (literally: **brothers and sisters**) does not belong to God.

17. Revelation 1:9: I, John, am **your brother** and your partner in suffering and in God's Kingdom and in the patient endurance to which Jesus calls us.

If Jesus's intention behind establishing his church was for it to mimic a surrogate family, where its members are akin to loyal, committed, first-century sibling relationships, are we able to say that describes our current church culture?

BEYOND CHURCH ATTENDANCE

Church is not an event you attend or content you consume but a family to which you belong. Any other approach to church flies in the face of Jesus's vision for the greatest friend group we could have that can draw us closer to one another and God himself. Hellerman drives it home when he writes,

> By separating salvation from church involvement, in a culture that is already socially fragmented and relatively devoid of relational commitment, we implicitly give people permission to leave God's family when the going gets rough—to take their personal relationships with Jesus with them to another church down the block or, worse, to no church family at all. . . . We have removed from the gospel what the Bible views as central to the sanctification process, namely, commitment to God's group. In doing so, we invariably set ourselves up for the relational shipwrecks that happen in the lives of countless Sunday attenders who opt for individual satisfaction over loyalty to God's group. After all, "I can leave my church—or my marriage—and my personal Savior will happily accompany me where I go." . . . To leave God's family is to leave the very arena in which God manifests His life-giving power and hope to human beings in the world in which we live.[167]

Granted, we don't live in first-century collectivist Palestine, and it is impossible and impractical to fully think we can in our twenty-first-century individualist context. Regardless, at the very least, we have to move beyond the notion that mere church attendance is optional for our spiritual formation and sense of belonging.

In his book *Faith for Exiles*, David Kinnaman and Mark Matlock highlight the faith practices and values of the 10 percent of eighteen-to-twenty-nine-year-old Christians who remain deeply engaged with their faith and churches. He calls this 10 percent "resilient disciples," whose vibrant faith is a stark contrast to the 59 percent of young Christians who drop out of the church after high school. One of the distinctive characteristics of resilient disciples is they find meaningful belonging in their local church. The statistics below show the percentage of resilient disciples who strongly agree with each of the following statements:

- *The church is a place where I feel I belong*: 88 percent.
- *There is someone in my life who encourages me to grow spiritually*: 85 percent.
- *I am connected to a community of Christians*: 82 percent.
- *When growing up, I had close personal friends who were adults from my church, parish, or faith community*: 77 percent.
- *I admire the faith of my parents*: 72 percent.
- *I feel emotionally close to someone at church*: 64 percent.[168]

Now, you might be thinking these young adults just so happened to find a church that made them feel like they were at home. And perhaps that's possible. But what's most startling about these statistics of resilient disciples' responses is they range anywhere from 30 to 80 percent higher in comparison with their less devoted Christian peers. Experiencing belonging and community in a local church has less to do with finding "the perfect church" and everything to do with committing to the church you find. Active belonging and participation in the local church are core components to a thriving faith and life in Jesus, plain and simple. Therefore, we need to start leaning in to the sibling-like bonds we can have with the spiritual friends within our churches. This is a major step toward reclaiming our God-given design for community and remedying our loneliness for good.

So how do we that? Here are some practical ways for how we can move beyond church attendance in the public space and start getting to know the brothers and sisters you never knew you had.

1. FIND A LOCAL CHURCH.

If you haven't found a local church to call home yet, this is the place to start! All it takes is a simple Google search to see the churches in your area. Browse their websites to get a feel for who they are, learn about their beliefs, and figure out what you can expect on a Sunday morning. Their websites often include links to other ministries, like their kids' ministries for your children to attend, small groups, serving teams, and the like. Further, you can normally access the church's social media accounts from their website, as well as their YouTube, Vimeo, or podcast accounts. This is a great way for you to get an idea of what the church is like before you step foot through the door.

But the key is to actually step foot through the door.

This is the most intimidating part for people, because many of us don't like showing up to large groups as strangers. That's why I think so many people just opt for consuming the church's content online in the comfort of their isolated fortress they call home. But just like we talked about in chapter 4, connecting to a church while isolated will always be the more comfortable option—but it will not give you community. So try bringing a friend or two along with you to check out the church. That makes it a lot less intimidating.

2. "DATE" THE CHURCH.

The search for a local church is often called "church shopping." But I like to refer to it as "church dating." (Hear me out, okay? This is a metaphor.)

Local churches act like friends in a lot of ways. There are some people we connect with right away who become our immediate best friends from the start. But then there are others with whom a little more "work" on our end is required to develop a friendship (you know exactly what I'm talking about). The connection just isn't as natural, or you know they're someone where, for your own health (let alone sanity), you can't allow the relationship to move beyond a good acquaintance. While we are called to *love* everyone, even those we don't naturally connect with, not everyone has to be a close friend to whom we pour out our guts and around whom we can be our most vulnerable selves. In fact, we shouldn't do that with everyone we meet. Even Jesus didn't do that.

It's the same thing with churches. Churches aren't just buildings, or religious institutions, or even a collection of individuals. They are more like one collective person. That's super hard for our individualistic minds to comprehend. Every individual church member is part of the collective church person, otherwise known as the "one body of Christ." So when you encounter the collective church person of a local congregation, it really is like you're befriending someone.

Church shopping, then, becomes a lot more like church dating. We're called to love everyone, befriend most of them, get really close to some of them, and marry one of them (if we're called to marriage), just like Dunbar's circles of friendship show. The exclusivity of one spouse means you better do the hard work to know they're the right person to commit the rest of your life to. You need to make sure they share the same values, your personalities mesh well, you have similar dreams for your family, you can find middle ground on your finances, let alone be attracted to them. Do we call that "person shopping"? Of course not! It's doing the hard work before you enter into the most vulnerable relationship you'll ever have. (Disclaimer: the whole act of "dating" to find a spouse is still a super Westernized act of individualism, but that's a conversation for another day.)

It's the same thing with churches. Granted, if you're looking for a church only for the amenities, like great music, flashy lights and lasers, preaching style, aesthetics, donuts, and an in-house coffee shop—basically anything apart from relationships—then you're absolutely church shopping. It's no different from buying a house at that point. But if you're looking at churches to find a culture that embraces you, a mission you believe in, a community you can belong to, and friends who want to know you, then you're searching for belonging, not church shopping.

Shopping for churches is an act of consumerism. Searching for belonging is an act of humanity. Though it's impossible to find the perfect church, it's important we do the hard work to find the right church. And when you find the right church, commit to them. Make church attendance a priority! But don't just settle for the weekly worship event. As you attend the church more and more frequently, that's when you should move to step 3.

3. MEET SOMEONE NEW.

This seems so basic that it shouldn't even have to be mentioned, but it can be so easy for our individualistic and isolated lifestyles to arrive to service late, sit by ourselves, and leave early before anyone has the chance to say hi. Perhaps the simplest way for us to break those tendencies is to introduce ourselves to someone we've never met before. Try sitting by someone else who's there by themselves, or just make it a point never to sit alone in church. Churches often have a time where you can turn and greet your neighbor. Extroverts love this, while it's every introvert's nightmare, but regardless—take advantage of that moment to meet someone new and share snapshots of your lives. Personal and intimate spiritual friendships all start with that initial "Hello, what's your name?"

Additionally, many churches have connection centers where you can give them your contact information and learn about how you can plug in deeper to meet more people. Talk with those staff members and volunteers at those stations, and they will be happy to help you find community.

4. ARRIVE EARLY AND STAY LATE.

Another step you can take is to arrive early to service and stay late. Make it a point to show up ten, fifteen, maybe even thirty minutes early just so you can talk with people before service starts while you sip your ~~terrible-tasting, creamer-infused, wow-I-should-have-gone-to-Starbucks-instead~~ church coffee. Then, stay a little while after service ends. A phrase we say at the end of every service at Resilient Church is, "Don't rush out the door, but rush to meet one another." What do you have to do that's so important after church anyway? Take that time to talk a little bit more with the new person you just met or to spend some extra time with your spiritual friends you're gradually getting to know. This is such a simple way to start developing these spiritual friendships with your brothers and sisters in Christ.

5. GET INVOLVED.

Another step you can take that grows you closer to your brothers and sisters in the church is to get involved. There are so many ways you can move beyond mere church attendance at your church. One example includes Sunday morning serving teams. Many churches have teams you can join that help with various parts of the service, like parking lot attendants, coffee and refreshments, administration, kids' ministry, tech and media, worship music, security teams, marketing and communications, outreach, and so much more. One obvious benefit is you get to help the church run. You become a part of something bigger than yourself. But the other incredible benefit of getting involved with church serving teams is rubbing shoulders with others who love the church and Jesus. Serving teams become little church families of their own who look forward to serving together when their rotation comes around and who also take time to pray together. They are a great way to start forming more entry-level spiritual friendships in the social space.

Another way you can get involved is to join a class. Churches often have short-term classes you can join that provide great information that can aid you in your walk with Jesus, while also developing friendships with others who are on a similar journey. Again, the goal for joining a class shouldn't be just to learn the information but also to meet new people in a more interactive environment that can help foster the development of spiritual friendships.

6. MEET UP DURING THE WEEK.

As I said in chapter 7, the key difference between social friends and personal friends is you do additional activities together outside your normal meeting places. So another step you can take is to extend an invitation to someone to meet up during the week, just like how I asked Damian to move our spiritual friendship from the social space to the personal space over Vietnamese cuisine. Is there someone you've started to click well with on your serving team that you would love to get to know more? Or is there a group of you that keeps gravitating toward each other on Sundays, but nothing ever develops beyond that? Offer to meet up during the week! Invite her out to coffee, have him over for dinner, or host a game night with your newfound spiritual friends. These conversations don't even have to be about anything explicitly spiritual, either. It's just a chance to get to befriend another brother or sister at a more personal level than what you may have right now.

7. JOIN A SMALL GROUP.

Another crucial step you can take to move beyond church attendance and develop spiritual friendships is to join a small group. They can go by a myriad of different names, like Life Groups, Community Groups, Discipleship Groups, or just simply Small Groups. Regardless of the name, these "smaller groups" are often the primary vehicle for church members to develop close-knit community with one another. They often consist of seven to twelve people, though they can be more or fewer than that, and typically meet on a weekly basis in someone else's home. They may start with small talk about how everyone's week has been going, all while munching on some snacks or a meal. From there, the large majority of the time spent in a small group is to discuss God's truth and how it applies to the members' lives. They may do this through a Bible study, a video curriculum, or a book, discussing what parts of their lives can change or adapt to live out God's will for their lives more faithfully.

The key to being a part of an effective small group is to commit to it for *at least* a year. Everyone starts out in the social space at first, and it could take a full ten to twelve weeks before everyone starts to feel really comfortable with each other. But after those first three months, that's when the benefit of these groups can really start to take off. I've been a part of my current small group for a little over a year now, and our spiritual friendships with one another are the most fruitful they've ever been. *But it took time.* So when you join a group, commit to stay beyond the first three months.

———

To recap, a lonely Christian is a contradiction, because there is no such thing as an "only child" in God's family. According to the New Testament and Jesus's vision for the church, we are not just saved from eternal damnation and rescued from our sins, but we are also adopted into God's family as his sons and daughters. We cannot be dynamic followers of Jesus without being an active participant in his church. Therefore, that requires us to lean in to our brothers and sisters in Christ and commit to them with the undivided loyalty that was assumed of first-century sibling relationships. Although it's impossible for us to duplicate the exact lifestyle of the early church in their cultural context, the least we can do is move beyond mere church attendance and content consumption and start befriending our brothers and sisters. To review, here are the seven simple steps we can take with our church families:

1. Find a local church.
2. "Date" the church.
3. Meet someone new.
4. Arrive early and stay late.
5. Get involved.
6. Meet up during the week.
7. Join a small group.

If you start doing these seven things, you will start to reclaim your God-given design for community and begin remedying your loneliness for good.

But there's still something missing.

All of these steps are great to start scratching the surface of our spiritual friendships. But they are not guaranteed to develop personal, and especially intimate, spiritual friendships. You can go to church every week, serve on a team, join a small group, and do all sorts of church activities to *get to know* all your new brothers in sisters in Christ *without ever being fully known.* The beautiful thing about families is they are supposed to be the groups who can know you and support you in a way that no one else can. But unfortunately, it's far too easy to belong to Christian community and hide the deepest, most vulnerable parts of ourselves. And that's why we can still belong to a church and feel lonely and isolated.

That's why we need to relearn how to be naked again.

DISCUSSION QUESTIONS

1. Do you have any siblings? What was your relationship like growing up? How are your sibling relationships unique from any other relationship you have?
2. What sticks out to you about first-century collectivist cultures and their family-oriented way of life? How do you think that way of life impacts the way the early church functioned?
3. What do you think cultivating a sibling-like bond with other believers at your church looks like?
4. Revisit the seven steps you can take to grow closer to your church family. What's a step you need to take?

CHAPTER 9

NAKED AND UNASHAMED

Therefore confess your sins to each other and
pray for each other so that you may be healed.

– James 5:16 –

In July 2018, I traveled back to my hometown for vacation in Richmond, Indiana. I set up shop one morning at Roscoe's Coffee Bar, one of my favorite local coffee shops back home, to spend some time with the Lord, read Scripture, journal, and so forth. Naturally, since I was drinking coffee, it was only a matter of time before my insides were on the move . . . if you know what I mean.

Eventually, I had to go do my business. And to my dismay, I clogged the toilet.

I mean, I *completely* clogged the toilet.

I was also working at a local coffee shop in Sioux Falls, South Dakota, at the time, so I knew from personal experience that there's nothing worse than going into the bathroom to discover that you have to deal with someone else's crap. So, as an act of charity toward my fellow baristas at Roscoe's, I took matters into my own hands and plunged the toilet myself.

Only for it to get even *more* backlogged.

I watched in utter horror as the water inched its way closer and closer to the edge of the bowl. All the while, I'm desperately praying, "Oh God, please do not let this overflow, oh God, please do not let this overflow, I'm literally going to die. HELP ME, LORD GOD ALMIGHTY. May this toilet not overfloweth in JESUS'S NAME!"

To the glory of God, it stopped.

But it gets worse. The worst part of this scenario was *not* that I clogged the toilet. Oh no. The worst part was that I had to *tell* the barista that I clogged their toilet.

Hear it from me: There is truly nothing more humbling and humiliating in this life than having to tell another human being, "I clogged your toilet."

So I shamefully walked to the register and confessed my travesty to the barista (who coincidentally was someone I knew from high school; his name was Dan). And all Dan said in reply was, "Well, it's been quite the start to my morning." He walked to the back of Roscoe's and returned with rubber gloves, armed and ready to take on my mess.

It was completely humiliating. But I share all this with you because there *is* a point to my poop story . . .

We need other people to help us handle our crap.

COVERED AND ASHAMED

As we discussed in chapter 2, Adam and Eve were designed for community by reflecting the relational nature of God. Adam was perfect, but incomplete; he was not fully human until he could live in communion with God *and* Eve. But a core quality of Adam and Eve's perfect relationship was that they could be naked and unashamed (Genesis 2:25). Yes, they were *physically* naked and unashamed, but they were also *emotionally* naked and unashamed. They could fully know and be known by each other and God with nothing to hide. They fully lived in each other's intimate space.

Yet, when Adam and Eve sinned against God and ate from the forbidden fruit, what happened? They were filled with shame, ran away in an attempt to hide from God, and covered themselves from each other (Genesis 3:8). When God found them and asked what they did, they ignored the issue and blamed each other.

Adam and Eve went from being naked and unashamed to covered and ashamed.

This is an ongoing strategy of God's adversary, Satan. The enemy knows we are most vulnerable if he can get us to cover our true selves and keep us alone in our shame. We want to hide when we encounter our sin, isolate when we feel shame, cast the blame on someone else, divert attention from our shortcomings, and suppress our brokenness at all costs.

Remember, loneliness and isolation are not necessarily the same thing. Loneliness can be imparted upon us against our will, whether that's due to the death of a loved one, transitioning during a new season of life, or dear friends moving away. Again, loneliness is our emotional "check engine" light that reminds us to connect with others in community, especially if we no longer have relationships like we once had before. Retreating into isolation, however, is an action we do to ourselves. We don't just isolate from others because we would rather be on social media or watch TV than hang out with our friends. That certainly contributes to our sense of loneliness, but it's the isolation that occurs from our shame and fear of our sin, emotions, actions, and any troubles in our life that tempts us to be like Adam and Eve—to cover up our "nakedness" and shield ourselves from being fully known.

Justin Whitmel Earley says, "Hiding begins as our unwillingness to be seen and then becomes our insistence not to be known—and that is the root of all loneliness."[169] That's precisely why shame continues to be an effective method for Satan to wreak havoc on our God-given design for community, because shame is an isolation powerhouse.

Brené Brown is one of the world's leading experts on shame. In her seminal work, *Daring Greatly*, she says, "Shame is the intensely painful feeling or experience of believing that we are flawed and therefore unworthy of love and belonging."[170] Brown contends that we are at our best psychologically, emotionally, cognitively, and spiritually when we are connected with others who make us feel loved and like we belong. Shame, on the other hand, is the fear of *disconnection*. It's the emotion we feel when we believe that there's something so wrong about us that deems us unworthy of love, or that we did something so awful that there is no way we will be forgiven, or that our identities are so askew that we will forever be alone. When we're ashamed, we assume no one wants to know how we truly feel, and we are thus afraid people will run away if they discover the real us. Brown says shame is a universal emotion—we all have it, we've all felt it, and we all struggle to talk about it.[171]

The reason shame is so powerful is because the brain literally registers the emotional pain of shame the same way it registers physical pain. It hurts. Shame triggers our survival instincts and puts us in a fight-or-flight mode, which is really effective when tending to threats, but they greatly hinder our ability to connect with others. This is why extensive amounts of shame that build up over time can lead to self-destructive behaviors like addiction, depression, and eating disorders, or attacking others through violence, aggression, or bullying.[172]

I don't think it's a coincidence that many of the symptoms of shame are synonymous with the symptoms of prolonged loneliness. Going into hiding and covering our true selves yields emotional disconnectedness, which only exacerbates our loneliness. What's fueling our world's loneliness epidemic isn't a vast amount of people living friendless lives or having excessive screen time while holing up in their isolated houses. It's because we're feeling unknown, drowning in our shame alone, left to handle our crap on our own. But instead of using fig leaves to cover our nakedness and shame like Adam and Eve did (Genesis 3:7), we use our personalized devices as numbing agents to cover our sin and nakedness *from ourselves*, let alone others. As the twentieth-century theologian Dietrich Bonhoeffer says, "He who is alone in his sin is utterly alone."[173]

So what's the solution? What do we do with this emotion that keeps us isolated and disconnected? What do we do with this devilish scheme of old that keeps us trapped in our shame?

Well, the solution lies within living out our originally intended design by our Creator.

We need to learn how to be naked again.

TO BE NAKED AND UNASHAMED AGAIN

No, I am not giving you permission to relive the glory days with your bros in your college fraternity. I mean we need to get *emotionally* naked. The way we overcome the isolating power of shame is simply to talk about it. Brown says,

> Shame derives its power from being unspeakable. . . . If we cultivate enough awareness about shame to name it and speak to it, we've basically cut it off at the knees. Shame hates having words wrapped around it. If we speak shame, it begins to wither. . . . [But] the less we talk about shame, the more control it has over our lives.[174]

So here's the kicker. It is precisely when we encounter a shameful experience where the crap hits the fan (or clogs your toilet) that we need to lean in to our friends, not isolate from them. This is exactly what God designed spiritual friendships to accomplish in our lives. But it's also what makes them so hard. Just because speaking our shame is simple doesn't mean it's easy. This is where our American culture and our God-given design for emotionally and spiritually naked community collide. Our consumeristic selves want that perfect, idealistic sense of community that meets our exact expectations without any problems whatsoever that's all fun, all pleasure, all the time. That's worldly friendship at its finest.

But true spiritual friendships fly in the face of consumerism because perfect community without people's problems just doesn't exist. Bonhoeffer identifies this problem as the "wish dream of Christian community." He says that anyone looking for a perfect, idealistic community with no problems, discord, discomfort, or mess simply will not find it. Such a community is only a "wish dream." Much to their surprise, it's actually the very presence of people's problems, dysfunction, discomfort, and mess that prove you're in authentic community![175] In other words, as soon as people start sharing about their shame and difficult life experiences, and things begin to feel uncomfortable and messy—*ding ding!*—congratulations, you have found community.

Unfortunately, our consumeristic, worldly ways urge us to retreat and isolate when we reach this point. Shame's power continues on because being vulnerable about our weaknesses is often viewed as a weakness in itself.[176] Throw in our culture's value of individualism, and it's even considered commendable if you can tackle all of life's problems alone! "Just pull yourself together and get it done," the world says. "You don't need anyone else."

But if we're honest, our resistance to participate in messy community where everyone can bear each other's burdens is more of a reflection on us than the community we are a part of. It's not those sharing their mess that's the problem but our inability to tend to them and listen. Further, if these people are able to share their mess, then that just might mean we have to share ours too. Or what if we're fine with others talking about their mess, but we think our mess is, well, messier? As if their sin and shame are easily forgivable, but we are too far gone? In his book *The Celebration of Discipline*, Richard Foster expounds on our difficulty with confession when he says,

> We all too often view the believing community as a fellowship of saints before we see it as a fellowship of sinners. We feel that everyone else has advanced so far into holiness that we are isolated and alone in our sin. . . . Therefore, we hide ourselves from one another and live in veiled lies and hypocrisy.[177]

As justified as those fears and concerns are, again, we need to look at the stats. We simply *cannot* handle our crap on our own unless we want to engage in self-destructing behaviors. The more we keep our shame and brokenness hidden and covered, the more likely we'll explode like a pressure cooker without the proper release of its steam. Bonhoeffer argues that it is through the discomfort and less than ideal elements of being gathered with a bunch of messy nitwits that sharpens us and grows us to look more like Christ. "Only that fellowship which faces such disillusionment," he says, "with all its unhappy and ugly aspects, begins to be what it should be in God's sight, begins to grasp in faith the promise that is given to it."[178] Iron sharpening iron is a painful process (Proverbs 27:17). Yet it is the tension of rubbing against other people's sin *together* that the Spirit of God uses to form us more into Christ's image. It's what being a part of the body of Christ is all about. The thing that draws us away from community, according to worldly friendship's standards, is the very thing that should draw us toward it. As the apostle Paul writes in his letter to the Galatians, "If another believer is overcome by some sin, you who are godly should gently and humbly help that person back onto the right path. And be careful not to fall into the same temptation yourself. Share each other's burdens, and in this way obey the law of Christ" (Galatians 6:1–2). I love how Justin Whitmel Earley puts it when he says,

> Everything changes when we realize that our instinct to hide is not only wrong but also incredibly dangerous. We mistakenly think that hiding keeps us safe by shielding us from danger. But what hiding actually shields us from is love. It may be counterintuitive at first, but consider that we are not happiest when we are hiding and "safe." We are happiest when we are exposed and loved anyway. We are the most human when we are most intimately known. And that means coming out of our hiding places.[179]

If we want to reclaim our God-given design for community and remedy our loneliness for good, we need to learn how to be "naked and unashamed" with God and our friends, just as it was intended since the Garden of Eden. We need to embrace each other's mess, share our burdens with our friends who stick closer than a brother or sister, and handle one another's crap as we journey into Christ's likeness and holiness *together*.

And the key to doing so is through regularly practicing confession and vulnerability.

THE POWER OF CONFESSION AND VULNERABILITY

James 5:16 tells us to "confess your sins to each other and pray for each other so that you may be healed." The truth packed into this one simple verse is unfathomable. Some may hear the word *confession* and think of getting a defendant to admit to a wrongdoing in a court case or going into a dark confessional booth with a priest at a Catholic church. But according to its long-running history in the Christian tradition, confession is a spiritual discipline of regularly confessing our sins to God and to others. It involves admitting to wrongdoing, disclosing harmful secrets, and being vulnerable with difficult emotions, all of which can lead to the reconciliation of relationships to live in harmony again. Confession isn't just a practice for righting a sinful action you committed against someone or God; it's the vulnerability of disclosing *anything* you would usually try to keep covered and hidden. And truly, doing so can be incredibly healing.

Brené Brown says vulnerability—speaking what we want to keep covered and hidden—is the antidote to shame. She says, "Vulnerability is the birthplace of love, belonging, joy, courage, empathy, and creativity. It is the source of hope, empathy, accountability, and authenticity. If we want greater clarity in our purpose or deeper and more meaningful spiritual lives, vulnerability is the path."[180] Since shame isolates us from people, shame is best healed *among* people.

That's why Brown says reaching out to others and talking about our hard feelings are two practices that help develop shame resilience.[181] We have to get (emotionally) naked.

When we practice confession and vulnerability, what we're doing is developing what is known as "secure attachments" with people who provide a "haven of safety" to help us regulate our emotions, manage distress, and gain support in our life. When you do this with your friends, you're developing what Todd Hall calls a "secure base" that gives you confidence to explore and express the intricacies of your life.[182] While a therapist or counselor can provide a safe haven for you to dig into the vulnerable parts of your life, they are also bound to you by a professional contract that *requires* them to do so. That's why relational satisfaction and meaningful social support occur when we are fully known, seen, and heard by our friends who freely choose "to be there and love us anyway," as Justin Whitmel Earley says.[183] And this is especially important when we experience suffering.

SUFFERING TOGETHER

Back in 2020 when my mental health was at its worst, one of the ways I coped was processing it with other people. My wife was one of them, of course, as she is my most intimate spiritual friend. Confessing all my hard feelings and toxic thoughts to her listening ear was very helpful, but she also came up with ideas to help me cope, like yoga, walks, and coloring in an adult Harry Potter coloring book while watching *The Princess Bride* and *Dumb and Dumber*. I never would've done any of those things if I were left to my own devices. But I also didn't *only* confide in Kasey. I FaceTimed with my two best friends from Sioux Falls once a month. I would meet up with Eddy Shigley, my boss at the time, to walk around the track and process my feelings. Tyler Johnson, my best friend from high school, Face-Timed with me almost every week to discuss the season of *Survivor* I was binging and our journeys through Brandon Sanderson's massive epic fantasy series, *The Stormlight Archive*. I needed my friends to help me through my suffering, but they could only help to the extent I was willing to be vulnerable.

We need others to help us through suffering. It's the only way we'll ever recover. Brené Brown recalled a study that found if rape and incest survivors keep their experiences secret, they experience more psychological damage than the inciting event itself by letting it fester and build up inside them. On the other hand, when the group of trauma survivors from the study did share their stories and experiences, their overall physical health improved, their stress hormones significantly decreased, and their doctor's visits decreased.[184] This is why, as Todd Hall argues,

> Suffering is meant to be faced in relationship. We all need people to walk alongside us on the journey of suffering. We know from research and our experience that social support plays a huge role in helping people cope with trials and eventually grow from them. You need people who are safe for you to express your true feelings about your pain. Close connections are a positive outcome for those who grow through suffering, but they are also a mechanism for it. This means you need to put effort into reaching out to people who can be with you in the midst of a painful time. . . . You may not be able to change the circumstances, but others will help you not feel alone in the midst of suffering. Even though it's difficult when you're going through a hard time, you need to do your part in reaching out and being vulnerable.[185]

It's as if confession and vulnerability can heal us.

SOUL SHARING

However, confession and vulnerability don't just require us to open up about the negative ways we feel about ourselves, confess our wrongdoing, or receive support while we suffer. This discipline is also a means for us to connect with our friends at the soul level. In so doing, our spirits "intermingle" with Christ and one another, as Aelred would say.[186] Ruth Haley Barton says that "the soul is the place where our truest desires make themselves known if we can learn how to listen [to it]."[187] It is in our souls where our deepest desires and longings reside, and where God connects with us and ministers to our needs through his Holy Spirit.

Soul sharing is what constitutes deep, intimate spiritual friendships. The term *deep* communicates an image of something being buried or kept below the surface that is not visible to everyone else. Therefore, deep friendships are the excavators who "dig into" the parts of our lives that usually remain covered and bring them to the surface for others to see. While that certainly includes the difficult parts of our lives we want to keep buried and hidden, it also includes the deep things of God and the experiences of our soul. Remember: Adam and Eve were also in relationship *with God*. Discussing God's character, reading Scripture, praying, worshipping, wrestling through difficult theological questions, dwelling in God's divine nature, sitting in his presence, and striving toward his definition of the good life are all deep concepts and practices that bear significant implications, not just on our own lives but on the quality of our friendships as well. It is truly a different caliber of friendship when you can freely share about both the deeply personal matters of your soul and the things of God *together*, as God originally designed it to be. Therefore, vulnerability also requires us to share about our experience of God with our spiritual friends as well.[188] In fact, doing so draws us even *closer* to our friends and deepens our sense of intimacy.[189]

CONFESSION AND VULNERABILITY CULTIVATE INTIMACY

I had four different sets of roommates throughout my four years of college. Josh was my roommate freshman year. He was a happy-go-lucky, ridiculously tall guy who just always added a bit of spunk to your day anytime you interacted with him. Other than not being a big fan of his laundry habits, Josh and I had a good relationship. However, despite *living* together, he and I barely talked with each other. He would set up shop on our futon and study all day. We would catch up about how life was going every now and again, but that was about it.

During my third year of college (which was technically my senior year credits wise), JC and D were my roommates, and we did a lot more together than Josh and I ever did. We grabbed meals together, they introduced me to the TV shows *Friends* and *Futurama*, we participated in dorm events together, and we hung out with the same group of friends. I was closer with JC and D because we shared more of our life together than I did with Josh.

Then there were Zach and David, my roommates for my fourth year of college when we started our master's of divinity program together. We were in an apartment off campus, so we were all navigating the new world of "adulting" and being responsible for our own spaces. We spent countless hours studying together and struggling through our graduate level course work. But we also did so many fun things together: having movie nights, cooking new meals, roasting coffee, driving forty minutes to Anderson, Indiana, for Skyline Chili, and playing Rocket League (it's a video game where you play soccer in flying cars—it's awesome!). But we also helped each other with our problems. For example, they helped me navigate not only my girl troubles but also a crisis of faith I was having at the time. That's why I was closer with David and Zach than I was with JC and D, because we shared even *more* of our life together.

Then there was Matt—my sophomore-year roommate. I went out of order and saved him for last for a reason. Matt and I are best friends. We originally met in our freshman orientation group, and he thought I was crazy because of how hyper I was during all of our icebreaker games (seriously, what's up with all my best friends initially thinking I'm crazy?). But we soon discovered that we were also in the same unit of our freshman dorm, and we slowly started to hit it off. We played Halo 4 on his Xbox 360 every night, adventured to Kokomo, Indiana, just so we could get Chipotle, participated in all the insane shenanigans and traditions of our freshman dorm, Bowman House, and spent the following summer on staff for SpringHill Camps. Due to our growing friendship freshman year, we decided to be roommates our sophomore year. We did even *more* stuff together as roommates than we did as freshmen, and cultivated this beautiful, sarcastic friendship where whenever we said, "I hate your guts," we knew the other meant, "I love you so much." But as good as all these things were, what set my roommate relationship with Matt apart from the rest was the extent of ourselves we could share. We would stay up late and have "pillow talk," where we talked about our faith, bemoaned our inability to get a girlfriend, and any other struggle we could think of. We would go on to be in each other's weddings.

Despite doing incredibly fun and exciting things with all four sets of my roommates, it was the level of vulnerability Matt and I were willing to share with one another that made us the closest.

The depth of your relationships depends on the depth of yourself you share. If only one of you shares the deep parts of your life, you're more of a counselor than you are a friend. But the more you *mutually* share about the deep, vulnerable parts of your life, the closer you will become. Justin Whitmel Earley says, "There is a depth friendship cannot go to until you know the real flaws of someone else. . . . What we hide pushes people away. What we share draws them in."[190]

Think back to the Friend Zone Matrix in chapter 7. All four of the spaces our relationships can be categorized as relate to how much of ourselves we are willing to share with those individuals. There's truly no other way you get closer to your friends than through vulnerability. A Bible study won't do that. Vacations won't do that. Eating dinner together, sitting around a bonfire, playing Mario Party, or living with a college roommate won't do that. As great as these shared activities are, they in themselves will not deepen your friendships. So does that mean we can't do these activities with our deep, spiritual friends, if all we're meant to do is talk about our sin and shame together? Absolutely not! Surface-level matters *still matter*. Playing basketball, watching *Lord of the Rings*, going to a spin class, and talking about your grandma's desserts are all necessary in cultivating friendships and making memories. But at the end of the day, the depth of your friendships is determined by the depth of yourself you're willing to share with them. As David Benner notes,

> Like many other forms of relationship, friendships do not tend to remain static. They evolve or devolve—grow or shrink. If a friendship deepens over time, intimacy increases in depth and breadth. In fact, growth in intimacy is one of the best measures of growth in a friendship. In contrast, a sure sign of a dying friendship is a decrease of intimacy.[191]

BREAKING THROUGH TO COMMUNITY

Bonhoeffer's words regarding the power of confessing our sins and being vulnerable with what we want to keep hidden summarizes this chapter so well. He says,

> In confession the break-through to community takes place. Sin demands to have a man by himself. It withdraws him from the community. The more isolated a person is, the more destructive will be the power of sin over him, and the more deeply he becomes involved in it, the more disastrous is his isolation. Sin wants to remain unknown. It shuns the light. In the darkness of the unexpressed it poisons the whole being of a person. . . . In confession the light of the Gospel breaks into the darkness and seclusion of the heart. The sin must be brought into the light. The unexpressed must be openly spoken and acknowledged. All that is secret and hidden is made manifest. It is a hard struggle until the sin is openly admitted.[192]

It is through confession that we are no longer alone in our sin. In fact, it is only through confession that we can "find fellowship for the very first time."[193] This is when "the break-through" to community and spiritual friendship occurs: when we can come out of hiding and be *fully known* by our friends and God. Justin Whitmel Earley emphasizes this when he says, "Vulnerable community is the only real version of Christian community. You cannot have real community without real vulnerability."[194]

––––––––

This is how spiritual friendship is uniquely positioned to remedy feelings of loneliness in a time when so many Americans are severely lacking these close friendships. They are friends who know you intimately, as God knows you intimately. Granted, we will never, ever, ever come even remotely close to the infinite intimacy God has with us. He knows us more thoroughly than we know ourselves. But we're still not meant to be lonely with God.[195] Our spiritual friends can at the very least mimic God's intimacy with us when we can practice the vulnerability required of friends in the personal and intimate spaces.

All this is great. Confession and vulnerability are powerful means of healing our brokenness and drawing us closer to our friends and God. But the only way to receive this depth of relational satisfaction through confession is to actually do it—and to do so *regularly*. And as you can probably imagine, getting into a habit of regularly talking about our hardships with our friends is, well, hard.

That's why we need a system of structured vulnerability to practice confession regularly until the habit is so deeply ingrained into our psyches that it would be harder to isolate from our friends than it would be to confess our struggles to them.

DISCUSSION QUESTIONS

1. Recall a time in your life when you were ashamed from something and struggled to be vulnerable about it. What were the thoughts and feelings that accompanied the situation?
2. Now recall a time in your life when you were able to confess and be vulnerable about a shameful experience. What were the thoughts and feelings that accompanied that experience?
3. What are your general thoughts and feelings about regularly practicing confession and vulnerability with your close friends? Why do you think and feel the way you do?
4. Check your pulse on your comfort level regarding sharing about the vulnerable moments of your life with your friends. What conditions need to be present for you to feel comfortable sharing about these moments with them?
5. Now is a great time to practice vulnerability with your friends. Is there anything you need to confess and get off your chest right now?

CHAPTER 10

HOW IS IT WITH YOUR SOUL?

The heartfelt counsel of a friend is as sweet as perfume and incense. Never abandon a friend— either yours or your father's. When disaster strikes, you won't have to ask your brother for assistance. It's better to go to a neighbor than to a brother who lives far away.

– Proverbs 27:9–10 –

"How is it with your soul?"

As a group member of a Methodist class meeting in the 1700s, you would have been required to answer this question every single week. Class meetings consisted of eight to twelve people, all mixed in age,

202 • YOU NEED FRIENDS

social standing, and spiritual maturity. Each meeting began with singing a hymn, and then the class leader began sharing about the condition of his or her soul from the previous week. She would share what went well, what challenges she faced, how she was tempted to sin, how she actually fell into sin, and anything else she needed to confess. After the leader shared, everyone else would go in a circle and share about their lives in a similar fashion.

This small group structure was revolutionary for its day. It wasn't focused on reading books or discussing curriculum, like so many small groups are structured in churches today. Instead, Class meetings systematically required its members to confess regularly what was going well and what wasn't going well, and to hold each other accountable to holy living every single week.

However, if you wanted to go even deeper, you could join a Methodist Band meeting. Bands consisted of only four to six people of the same sex, marital status, and age group. Unlike Class meetings, Bands were optional (probably because they were more intense). The purpose of Bands was to get extremely vulnerable about your life so you could live more in accordance with God's Word. During a Band meeting, you were *required* to answer the following five questions every single week:

1. What known sins have you committed since our last meeting?
2. What temptations have you met with?
3. How were you delivered?
4. What have you thought, said, or done, which you doubted whether it was sin or not?
5. Is there anything you desire to keep secret?[196]

Members asked additional probing questions of each other to get as much of their life out into the light as they could, and then they concluded the Band meeting by praying over each other.

Talk about intense! Who would sign up for something like this? But the early Methodists took these two types of small groups seriously because they knew regularly practicing confession and vulnerability transformed their lives while drawing them closer to God and each other. They created a structure that ensured these things happened.

Sadly, far too many churches don't even offer small groups remotely close to the structure of the Methodist Class and Band meetings. As I alluded to in chapter 8, small groups can be a fantastic way to grow in your faith and learn more about God with a group of friends. But unfortunately, the spiritually formative communities of small group ministries are often vastly overpromised and under-delivered. As Ruth Haley Barton reflects in her book *Life Together in Christian Community*, "How often have we sat through inspiring sermons about what is possible when Christians gather together in mutually edifying relationships, only to recognize how cynical we have become after many failed attempts?"[197] I believe the reason this happens is because many small groups are structured around dis-cussing content as the ultimate end goal. Group members can read a book or a Scripture passage and discuss its contents and how it applies to their lives, and they will certainly grow in their friendships with one another while learning a thing or two about the Christian life over time. But this approach to small groups does not guarantee that you'll develop personal and intimate spiritual friendships. It's assumed discussing Christian content will grow you closer together, at least in terms of moving from strangers in the public space to friends in the social space. But as we just discussed, it's vulnerably sharing, confessing your hardships, and suffering well together that grows you closer together.

How a small group ministry is structured yields a certain type of friendship, and rarely is spiritual friendship the definitive end goal of many churches' small group ministries. A hunger for deep community is always desired in a small group, but group members rarely have the language of spiritual friendship to define what satisfying that hunger looks like. Even if spiritual friendships *do* form in small groups, it's often by accident, all without the individuals knowing that these friendships are true Intimate-Spiritual friendships! In his book *Sacred Companions*, David Benner observes that current small group approaches usually awaken people's hunger for spiritual friendship but often fail to satisfy it.[198] It's like getting a waft of a delectable dinner at a five-star restaurant but never getting to enjoy the meal.

Confession and vulnerability are so good for us, but admittedly they are so hard to practice on our own initiative. And if small group ministries are rarely designed with the end goal of cultivating intimate, vulnerable, spiritual friendships, then perhaps what we need is another approach to small groups within our churches that does just that.

And they're called spiritual direction groups.

INTRODUCING SPIRITUAL DIRECTION GROUPS

There are many resources out there that talk about spiritual direction groups, but two of my favorites are David Benner's work on spiritual accompaniment groups in his book *Sacred Companions* and Alice Fryling's work on group spiritual direction in her book *Seeking God Together*. These are two leading methodologies for small groups with the intentional goal of cultivating spiritual friendships where you can be fully seen, known, and heard.

First, what is spiritual direction? Individual spiritual direction involves companioning with another person, usually a trained spiritual director, to receive God's guidance and transformational work in your life.[199] Your spiritual director actively listens and prays on your behalf while you share whatever is on your mind, and then he or she asks you pointed questions about how God is present in the midst of your situation. It sounds a lot like spiritual counseling at first, but the focus isn't just to provide a space for you to talk about your hardships. Rather, the focus is on guiding you to see how God is uniquely present in the midst of your life circumstances and what he may be leading you to do next.

Group spiritual direction, then, takes the core practices of individual spiritual direction but applies them with three to five people over the course of one to two hours. Unlike traditional small groups that study the Bible or study a curriculum, spiritual direction groups emphasize members sharing about recent life experiences and how they may (or may not) be encountering God in the midst of them.

There are several ways to go about running a spiritual direction group, but here's an adapted format highly inspired by Alice Fryling's approach to these groups that I used for my dissertation research on how practicing spiritual friendship can remedy feelings of loneliness. We continue to use this group format in our church (we call them Spiritual Friend Groups), and they are a powerful way to draw people closer to each other *and* to God. Here's a basic overview of the structure.

Each group meeting begins with members spending the first fifteen to thirty minutes just catching up on life, typically over a meal, snacks, or drinks. When it's time for the session to start, the group begins with three to five minutes of prayerful silence after reading a short scripture, centering the group of friends on Jesus's presence in their shared space.

After this moment of centering, each member takes turns sharing, for five to ten minutes straight, about whatever has been going on in his or her life since their last meeting, while the others listen attentively without any interruptions. After a brief prayerful silence once the friend finishes sharing, the other group members respond not with advice but with deep questions about where God is found amid the sharing friend's situation. This is similar to the questions that Band and Class meetings would ask of their members. After this time of question and response, the next friend shares, always with a moment of prayerful silence to mark the transition to members asking questions, until everyone has fully shared.[200] Finally, group members conclude their meeting by praying for one another.

That's the basic structure of how to run a spiritual direction group. Now, let's dive deeper into five key features to set you up for success in how to run a group like this with some of your own spiritual friends.

1. OPEN SHARING

The first feature is open sharing. The point of these conversations is for you to share vulnerably about deeply personal matters to discover what God is doing in them, together with your friends. Confession of sins, processing convictions, wrestling with doubts, and major life decisions can all be discussed during a session. Now, opening up and talking about your life for ten minutes straight might feel rather uncomfortable at first. But participants in my study found that it gets more comfortable the more often they did it, and often found a release after doing so.

But in order for open sharing to occur, these groups must be a safe haven built on trust with the commitment to keep in confidence whatever is shared.[201] As Fryling suggests, spiritual direction groups must foster an atmosphere of love and acceptance where no one needs to fear being judged or condemned for what they present.[202] And as Aelred contends, the love of God and neighbor is at the heart of spiritual friendships, and that love will foster the safe space for deep spiritual experiences to be shared.

Furthermore, this is why members should exercise discretion when inviting someone into a spiritual direction group like this. Per Aelred's suggestion, not all friendships guarantee the pursuit of what is good and holy, and not everyone (even those who are sincerely devout in their allegiance to Christ) is trustworthy to receive this kind of sharing. Benner suggests praying for God's discernment about whom you could invite into a spiritual direction group like this.[203]

Lastly, I strongly suggest incorporating a meal into your spiritual direction group gathering. There's something about communing over food that helps build camaraderie, especially when it comes to the discussions that take place in these groups. Jesus even disclosed his pending betrayal over a meal. This could include light snacks, warm drinks, or a potluck.

2. ACTIVE LISTENING

The second feature of spiritual direction groups is active listening. The presenting member gets five to ten minutes to share whatever he or she wants with *no interruptions*. During that time, the other members actively listen without making comments or passing judgment. Fryling notes that those listening in a spiritual direction group are "second in command" to the one sharing. Active listening requires an "open spirit" where we are quick to find understanding without trying to solve problems, make suggestions, or provide answers. She says, "When we listen with open spirits, we allow our friends to be where they are without judgment and we invite them to experience grace in their present circumstances."[204]

If group members are to respond to the friend sharing, they are to do so with clarifying questions that help them better understand the friend's circumstances. This is why the end goal of spiritual direction groups is *not* to give advice or solve problems, but for members to walk away with the assurance that they are loved and supported, all while finding God in the midst of their situation.[205] As Bonhoeffer says,

> The first service one owes to others in the fellowship consists in listening to them. . . . Christians so often think they must always contribute something when they are in the company of others, that this is the one service they have to render. They forget that listening can be a greater service than speaking.[206]

It's also uber important to eliminate any potential distractions that will hinder you from actively listening to whoever is sharing. This especially means silencing your phones and watches. In fact, I suggest turning them off and putting them in another room entirely. Doing so will greatly increase your ability to pay attention to what is being shared. One of the greatest presents you can give someone is your undivided attention and presence. Active listening plays a bigger role in developing and deepening your friendships than you think.

3. CONTEMPLATIVE PRAYER

The third feature of spiritual direction groups is contemplative prayer, which "means [to focus our] awareness on God" as well as "to view with continued attention, to observe thoughtfully, and to consider thoroughly and to think deeply."[207] Contemplative prayer in spiritual direction groups involves the members simultaneously attuning their attention to Christ as they actively listen. Or as David Benner explains, it is "the continuous looking back and forth between God and the other person."[208] As you are listening to a friend processing a difficulty in her marriage, you are also contemplatively praying in your mind, *God, where are you in this? God, help my friend in this. God, reveal your healing presence.*[209]

This can be a large leap in our prayer life if we've never done this before. We often practice prayer in three ways: bowing our heads and closing our eyes while listening to someone else pray; praying silently or out loud whenever we are by ourselves; or praying out loud for someone else. But rarely do we pray silently *while another person is sharing.* It requires dual mental/spiritual action on our part to pray silently to God as we listen to the needs of our friend. But doing so is a tangible way of acknowledging Christ's presence in our midst. If Christ is truly with us when we are gathered with our friends, then we should be communing with him in prayer at the same time, shouldn't we?

4. ASKING DEEP QUESTIONS

Contemplative prayer and active listening lead to the fourth—and perhaps the hardest—feature of spiritual direction groups: asking deep questions. When the group member is finished sharing, the others are free to respond by asking questions centered only around where God is present in what has been shared. In spiritual direction groups such as this, Fryling says that "the goal is not to answer life's questions. The goal is to draw closer to God in the midst of the questions. Many times, it is in embracing our questions that we move more deeply into God's love."[210] Therefore, members should ask questions that allow the friend sharing to search for God in a deeper way. Deep questions of our souls are hardly ever easily answered but are rather explored with our spiritual friends to aid us in our search for those answers. So even when your friend asks, "Why would God allow me to lose my job?" you do not rush to answer the question or give advice. Instead, you and your friends sit in it, pray contemplatively, and respond by asking him, "Well, Chris, why do you think God *would* allow such a thing? Where do you think he is in this?"[211] Ultimately, the questions asked should be centered around where God is present in the situation or the inner spiritual experience of the friend. There's an odd comfort in having your friends be able to say, "We don't know the answer to that, but we're still with you."

Justin, one of my interviewees, said, "[I learned how] to let people ask me questions and kind of work through things myself. And then the same on the other end . . . I think that was one surprise or new area of feeling equipped there, is that friends don't have to just give advice and listen, but they can also ask questions to make me figure it out myself." Asking questions empowers the person sharing to come up with solutions themselves, and they are more likely to follow through on those solutions because they have a larger sense of ownership having come up with it themselves. Have you ever been given advice that was completely at odds with how you wanted to handle the situation? Asking questions releases the pressure from us having to solve our friends' problems and positions us to be more a supportive presence, while helping them discern their own next steps. This seems counterintuitive because sometimes we just so *desperately* want to help our friends by telling them what they should do. But pause, resist the temptation, and ask deep questions. It's surprisingly more impactful than you may think.

After a time of asking questions, then—and only then—the group members may ask the friend sharing if he or she would like any advice or insight on the matter. This is incredibly important to ask for the friend's permission first. Sometimes we aren't looking for answers or advice as we explore life's hardships; we just need the loving presence of friends who can hear us and help us process. But there are also times when we really want advice from friends we trust. That's why it is important to let the sharing friend decide if they would like any advice, and if they do, limit advice giving to about five minutes before moving to the next person.

5. SYSTEM AND STRUCTURE

The final feature of spiritual direction groups comes down to the nitty gritty details of the system and structure to set up and run a group like this.

Creating Spiritual Direction Groups. If a church happens to offer groups like this, it would be as easy as signing up on their website. But alas, many churches just don't have groups like this readily available to join. What this means is you may have to select and invite two to four of your own friends to join a spiritual direction group. Prayerfully discern the people God has placed in your life whom you deeply trust to hold your confessions in confidence and walk with you. Some prefer to do these groups with members of the same gender, although it's not necessarily required.

Location. Once you have a group of friends, select a location, time, and day. The location should be a place that's private so conversations can't be overheard by those outside the group. A living room or dining table at one of your homes is preferred to a coffee shop or restaurant in public. The privacy and intimacy of a home helps cultivate privacy and intimacy with your spiritual friends.

Time and Day. Next, select a time and day that works for everyone. It can be during breakfast, over lunch, or after the kids go to bed. It's good practice to allow thirty minutes or so of casual conversation at the beginning, perhaps over a meal, light snacks, or tea, before diving into the discussion. Allot 90 to 120 minutes for the discussion, since each member gets up to twenty minutes altogether to share about their life and respond to questions. While spiritual direction groups can meet weekly, Benner suggests groups like this meet every two weeks for two hours at a time, as it allows for enough spiritual and life experience to take place between meetings, and two hours is ample time for everyone to share.[212] If you would prefer meeting weekly, you can rotate every week between following the spiritual direction group structure and just doing life together, like a game night, movie night, playdates with the kids, and so forth. This rhythm especially helps you bond over the more surface-level matters of life while having fun together, which in turn makes connecting over the deeper, more serious matters that much easier.

Regarding Virtual Spiritual Direction Groups. If there was one thing that COVID-19 showed us it's that we can utilize Zoom—a platform originally designed for virtual business meetings—for *any* form of meeting, including Bible studies and small groups. Maybe you look at your current season of life and feel like you would be better able to create a virtual spiritual direction group over Zoom (or whatever your video platform of choice is) with closer friends who live out of town. This is absolutely better than nothing! However, just remember that it's still virtual. Our bodies are hardwired to connect with people in person; that's why we get so exhausted after too many video calls. So while you do get the benefit of regularly confessing your life with friends on a virtual call, you will miss out on the benefit of meeting with others in person (such as receiving a much-needed hug or a pat on the back).

Facilitator Structure. Unlike most small groups where there is one designated leader who guides the discussion, spiritual direction groups can rotate group facilitators. The facilitator is responsible for opening the session with a short Scripture reading and moment of silence, and then he or she will maintain an appropriate balance of talking, listening, silent prayer, and managing the flow of sharing. They are aware of the clock, reminding each member how much time they have left to share and answer questions to help move things forward so everyone has the chance to share. Finally, the facilitator closes the session by inviting members to pray for one another for ten to fifteen minutes over what was shared and identifies who will facilitate at the next meeting.[213]

Spiritual Direction Group Guide. Check out Appendix A for the Spiritual Direction Group Guide that gives a brief overview of the group structure that we discussed in this chapter as well as a list of questions you can use during your group sessions. This can serve as an aid for you as you start meeting with your newly formed spiritual direction group!

THIS WORKS

As I mentioned in the introduction, I put all of this to the test when I conducted my study for my dissertation on a group of thirty young adults between the ages of eighteen and twenty-four. The ultimate aim of my study was to see if their rates of loneliness decreased and their sense of social support increased after participating in a ten-week program I called The Spiritual Friendship Cohort. They met as a large group for six weeks where they learned about much of the content discussed in this book. Then they practiced spiritual friendship in spiritual direction groups of three to five people for four weeks. Participants also took three surveys before and after the intervention that measured any quantitative changes in loneliness experience, social support, and spiritual friendship experience. I also interviewed eight participants before and after the intervention for qualitative data regarding their experience in these three domains.

The results were astounding.

After completing the ten-week program, the thirty-member cohort experienced a statistically significant decrease in loneliness; a statistically significant increase in social support, especially among their friendships; and a statistically significant increase in spiritual friendship experience. (If you're interested in the quantitative data from my study, check out Appendix B.) Additionally, all eight interviewees said they experienced loneliness less and made new friends as a result from participating in the program and these groups.

One of the central findings from my study was the role of vulnerability in participants' sense of social support and remedying feelings of loneliness. According to the interviews, there were several reasons why someone may feel lonely, whether that was due to being physically isolated from others when he or she is alone, moving to a new city due to a life transition, or feeling emotionally disconnected from a crowd or group. But the most common category of interviewees' responses regarding the cause of their loneliness (24 percent) pertained to not having people who could listen to them and understand them—to be fully known.

Conversely, the most common category of interviewees' responses regarding how they feel supported (30 percent) was when they did have people who could listen to them and enabled them to be vulnerable. Further, before participating in the study, interviewees suggested that sharing about deeply personal matters (50 percent of responses) and having a common faith in God (50 percent of responses) would satisfy their hunger for deeper friendships. Therefore, it's significant that 48 percent of interviewees suggested *after the study* that practicing vulnerability in their spiritual direction groups was the common cause for decreasing loneliness, and that 63 percent of responses suggested vulnerability was the leading cause for forming new friendships. Let's dig into some of the stories of my participants' experience.

Stewart, Justin, and Alex (again, all participants' names have been replaced with pseudonyms) noted in their interviews that they were all able to discover commonalities among their group, particularly with common struggles they could "tackle together," to use Stewart's words. Since these groups were places where they didn't have to be afraid of being judged, they learned how to open up about their lives, which formed trust between them, helped them grow strong bonds with each other, and made it easier to be vulnerable the next time.

After affirming the formation of new friends from the intervention, Shae pointedly said, "It's kind of hard not to make new friends when you're sharing vulnerable aspects of your life with each other." She commented that it was due to the unavoidable time of scheduled vulnerability with her group that allowed this happen. "If I have that time with anybody, I'm likely to become their friend, or they'd be my friend, or whatever."

Zach even shared a powerful example of how the vulnerable space of his group helped process the difficult decision to no longer attend the University of South Dakota the following semester:

> I had built up the courage to tell my parents that I'm not going to continue pursuing the degree I've been pursuing. And that entire line of thought came from talking it out with the people in the spiritual friendship group thing. And I was able to talk to my family about it, because I had talked to someone else first.

Perhaps loneliness decreased and social support increased because the nature of spiritual friendships allowed each friend to be naked and unashamed in the deep parts of their life, without fear that the others would judge or run away from their "nakedness."

Other comments were made by participants about the expediency of depth that developed in the friendships in these groups. Tyler said, "I became a lot closer to people *a lot faster* by talking about deep topics" (emphasis added). Isabella said, "My greatest takeaways are the value of being open with people and them being open and honest in return. That really builds a sense of community *quickly*" (emphasis added). Briana said, "Conversations were good and trust was established *quickly*" (emphasis added).

In his post interview, Stewart recalled how it took only a few weeks to develop a similar depth of friendship with his group members that took years to develop with a neighborhood friend growing up. He said, "It took years to make the progress that we [his group] had in these number of weeks." When asked to expound on the growth he experienced from his group, he said, "I've finally got some friends that I can actually invest in." He always had acquaintances and people he went to work or school with, but he did not "really have a lot of deep friendships." All in all, this spiritual direction group gave him deep friends, who he defined as "people he can contact whenever, and they will be there; who keep it real, do not sugarcoat things, and are not afraid to tell you what they think or feel." They are real with him and actually exercise that trust.

To bring this all home, here are some other participants' testimonies after practicing spiritual friendship in this way:

> The growth in friendship was great. We were able to grow closer to one another and come alongside one another through whatever circumstances we were facing. Having the other members of our group only be able to ask questions was a unique aspect to the friendship. It forced us to really evaluate and look to God in all circumstances good or bad which in the end grew our

friendship even more! This really works! Having a chance to talk with one another and grow not only together but together with Christ at the center! It was a unique experience, and we hope to continue it now that we have developed a deep supportive group! (Ali)

A big takeaway was that God is gathered with us when we were meeting. (Lynnette)

I loved the friendship cohort meetings as I process well when I speak out my feelings and my points of view. It helps me see outside of myself and provide clarity on God's movement in my life. (Stewart)

I found it very helpful to be able to verbally talk through things occurring in life and then also getting asked questions that center around God. Having the questions more God centered helped me to realize God is everywhere. At first it was difficult to want to talk about stuff going on in my life but then when I found relief and saw God present it became easier. (Jenny)

But the four-week group meetings for our small group was amazing. I feel like I have gained some lifelong friends and I feel like I've grown closer to God. (Alexandra)

I really enjoyed it; it enabled me to make new friends and have these deep and meaningful conversations. It allowed me to explore my faith in a new way and realize that I'm not alone in having issues with God and trying to navigate that. What went well was having that set time each week on a Sunday to meet up and talk about our lives, also everyone was invested in the program. . . . One of my biggest takeaways is that we can have these conversations about our faith, our struggles and praises and they don't have to be awkward, and I feel like this experience has equipped me with skills to be able to navigate those conversations both with people I know and those I don't know. I left this experience with a much stronger faith and connection with God via Jesus than I had at the beginning, and it helped me to start putting in that work into my faith via prayer, reading the

Bible, etc. It made me a better Christian and want to take the next steps in my faith. (Kyleigh)

I loved it, especially the last four weeks. It was hard for me to speak ten minutes without interruptions, but I felt a release after doing so. I know that I need to strive for spiritual friendships because they are far more fulfilling! (Jaden)

When we put God in the middle of our friendship, we can expect to see growth whether that's emotionally or spiritually. In addition, praying with one another can draw us closer as a friend and to God as well. (Alex)

Spiritual friends are absolutely necessary in our walk with Christ. . . . The groups were outstanding. I went in feeling there was no way I was going to see this as a positive. I didn't think that it was completely necessary to have time to talk and think out loud about myself to friends. But it has completely changed the way that I have viewed being a good spiritual friend. Some big takeaways that I had were: Sometimes all that is required of being a good friend is listening and not having to give advice. Asking questions about the presence of God is a great way to help think about solutions to problems. It is easier to not have to solve problems of another friend and puts less strain on the relationship. (Shawn)

A STRANGE WAY TO GROW IN FRIENDSHIP

You might be coming to the end of this book excited to give a group like this a shot. But you might also be left scratching your head, wondering, *Is this really what I have to do to reclaim my God-given design for community and remedy my loneliness for good?* The answer, in short, is no—you don't *have* to follow this type of group structure to grow in your spiritual friendships. But you *do* have to be regularly vulnerable with a select number of friends to deepen your friendships and receive the relational satisfaction that comes with that.

And being so vulnerable so regularly just doesn't come automatically to many of us. Hence the importance of a structure like this to take a practice that is so foreign to us and turn it into a habit that's automatic when we're with our deep spiritual friends.

Shae, one of my interviewees, commented extensively on how this group structure was the reason she was able to share anything in the first place and how unusual of a practice it is to grow in friendship with anyone:

> Carving out time to talk about actual things is the whole reason that anybody was able to share anything. Like, if you put all of us together and just said, "Deepen your friendship," we would not have done it this way. I'm sure nobody would have because it's like . . . this is a new structure for people. Nobody, I feel like at least that I know, has a friendship where they're like, "Okay, we're gonna hang out for an hour and a half, like twenty minutes, you talk about whatever you want to talk about. And then I'll talk about what I want to talk about." It's like, that's not a thing.

To Shae's point, most friendships go with the flow, and if they do experience moments of vulnerability, they either happen organically or whenever the need arises. Setting aside a regular time intentionally to be vulnerable about whatever they want to talk about is "not a thing" people do, as far as Shae knows (and I bet most of us would agree). She went on to say that if someone asked her, "How are you?" even as a spiritual person, she would still talk about how school is going and the normal everyday topics we talk about. But she would not immediately think to answer how she views what God is doing in her schoolwork, as the system of asking questions in her spiritual direction group required them to do.

———

This group structure is designed to help you be vulnerable. But the goal of the structure is to serve you, not serve the structure.

Perhaps after a few months of meeting with your spiritual direction group, you can take this practice and implement it into some of your other relationships outside your group. So the next time you catch up with your sister over FaceTime, grab coffee with a friend, or have your monthly playdate with your other mom friends and their kids, you don't just talk about the surface-level matters of life. You can be vulnerable about your circumstances, actively listen, and ask intentionally deep questions. The point of the system is to create the habits of vulnerability, confession, listening, prayer, and asking as normal parts of our lives and relationships. Now, this doesn't mean you should be deeply vulnerable with every single person you meet. There are some things you can only share with those who deeply know you. But you may have some friends who can know more about you than what you're currently sharing.

When you share the deep parts of yourself, don't be surprised by how deep your friendships grow.

DISCUSSION QUESTIONS

1. What is your initial reaction to following a structure in spiritual direction groups?
2. What part about spiritual direction groups sounds exciting to you? What part sounds difficult to you?
3. Spend time giving the spiritual direction group structure a shot. Refer to Appendix A as a guide.

CONCLUSION

Frodo can't do it any longer.

Having just evaded being eaten by a giant spider, escaped captivity by a group of orcs, and marched across the barren wasteland of Mordor without any water, Frodo collapses on the slope of Mount Doom—the fiery volcano into which he must cast the one Ring of Power to destroy the Dark Lord, Sauron. He just lies there, faint, so close to finally finishing this mission . . . but also so close to his death.

Thank goodness he isn't alone.

In that dark moment where all seems lost, with fiery balls of ash launching into the distance, his best friend, Samwise Gamgee, comes alongside him, holds him close, and encourages him.

"Do you remember the Shire, Mr. Frodo?" Sam asks. "It'll be spring soon. The orchards will be in blossom and the birds will be nested in the hazel thicket." Sam continues to remind Frodo of all the beautiful memories of life back home: the summer barley in the fields, the taste of strawberries.

Frodo murmurs back, weakly, in response that he can't recall these things he once held so near and dear to him. He's surrounded by darkness. Hopeless. The enemy seems to have overtaken his life. He can't go on.

But rather than leaving Frodo in his despair, Sam looks him in the eye, and boldly declares, "Then let us be rid of it. Once and for all. Come on, Mr. Frodo. I can't carry it for you. But I can carry you."

Sam hulls Frodo onto his shoulders, and with a fierce look of determination, begins carrying Frodo up the slopes of the mountain.[214]

Gah. I'm crying just writing this.

If you've never seen *Lord of the Rings*, then I encourage you to watch this clip from the movie (I've even included a QR code for you to watch the clip). It makes me weep every single time I watch it because it so perfectly articulates the spiritual friendships we hunger for in our own lives. Someone who sits with us in

Frodo & Sam Clip

our darkest moments, reminding us of all the good things this life still has to offer and how good God still is. Although these friends can't carry our burdens for us, they can help carry us up our mountains.

This is what God designed us for. From the very beginning of humanity, God said, "It is not good to be alone." Loneliness is literally our biological "check engine" light programmed to remind us that we need friends. Extended periods of chronic loneliness wreak havoc on our bodies, minds, and souls, resulting in worsened mental health conditions, addiction, illness, and even early death.

Hence our noncontestable design for community. We are a social, gregarious species hardwired for love and belonging. Living in significant community results in better mental health, strengthened immune systems, healthier habits, and a stronger sense of purpose in this life. We are truly at our best when we do this life with others.

But unfortunately, living in interdependent community goes against the grain of our culture that perpetuates our increasingly lonely lifestyles. In a radically individualist culture where the self reigns supreme, it can be difficult to admit that we need anyone, let alone reveal our weaknesses to them. While many Americans say they are satisfied with their number of friendships, many are still hungering to be closer to their friends.

On the other side of the coin is our isolationist tendencies. People are opting for services that keep them in their homes and reducing interactions. No other device and service proliferates this isolationism more than the smartphone and social media, which is especially harmful to young adults' mental health, relational abilities, and loneliness levels. With these two forces at work, it is no wonder we're facing a loneliness epidemic.

But it doesn't have to be this way. In order to reclaim our God-given design for community and remedy our loneliness for good, it starts with befriending the greatest friend we could possibly have: Jesus Christ himself. Jesus, the Son of God, became one of us so he could dwell among us as his friends. But perhaps the greatest act of friendship occurred when he laid his own life down for us, by taking our punishment on the cross, to restore our friendship with God again. Now we no longer relate with God strictly in a vertical relationship where God is above us but also in a horizontal relationship where God is with us. We can be fully known by God because of Christ's death and resurrection, and in that sense, we are truly never alone because we have God's ever-present Holy Spirit accompanying us.

However, we are not meant to follow God alone. Since we are designed for community, our friends form us into who we are and who we're becoming. Therefore, St. Aelred of Rievaulx advises us to be wise in whom we befriend—to avoid the devastation that carnal friendships can bring to us, and to call our worldly friendships to something greater, beyond fun and pleasure. Spiritual friendship is the greatest good we can experience on this earth, because it is through friends mutually pursuing Jesus together that we can be formed into God's image. Spiritual friends allow us to receive God's love tangibly from others and give God's love to others.

What's just as important to the spiritual quality of our friendships, though, is acknowledging the depth of their friendship with us. The closer the friend, the stronger their formational power over our lives. So even if we are going to church and attending a small group, if our closest friends we spend the most time with are participating in carnal activities, so will we. It's very difficult to fully follow Jesus by ourselves. But if we can learn how to prioritize our closest friends to be mutual followers of Jesus, not only will we be more strongly formed into Christlikeness, but we will be better able to relate with those who don't know Jesus and invite them into relationship with him.

But where can we go to find these spiritual friends and begin developing closer relationships with them? Look no further than the local church. Despite more and more people thinking they can follow God on their own terms, Jesus formed his church to function as a group of surrogate siblings. Our fellow church members are our brothers and sisters because we all have been adopted into God's family. So committing to a local church and finding spiritual friends that stick close to us like a brother or sister is vital, whether that's through arriving early and staying late, volunteering on a ministry team, or joining a small group.

While church involvement will begin helping you develop spiritual friendships, what will take them deeper and draw you closer to others and God is learning how to be naked and unashamed together. Loneliness doesn't just come from being physically isolated but from not having people who fully know you and love you anyway. Your spiritual friends are meant to be safe havens where you can be vulnerable about your shame, confess your shortcomings, and bear your burdens with others and vice versa. The depth of your friendships is determined by the depth of yourself you share.

If we want closer spiritual friends who draw us closer to God and each other, then we have to regularly practice vulnerability and confession. However, doing so does not come naturally. That's why having a structure like a spiritual direction group can help us regularly meet with our close friends, talk about the matters weighing deeply on our hearts, actively listen to each other, and ask questions about how God is uniquely present. Whether a structure like this is followed or not, it is only natural for our friendships to get closer the more deeply of ourselves we regularly share while having Christ in our midst. When these bonds are experienced, the result is decreased feelings of loneliness, increased feelings in social support, and a deeper awareness of God's involvement in our lives.

And that is a bond which God would deem "very good" indeed.

APPENDIX A

SPIRITUAL DIRECTION GROUP GUIDE

1. Open with silence and Scripture. The leader appointed from the previous session begins with three to five minutes of silence. After the first couple of minutes of silence, the leader reads a short passage of Scripture of his or her choosing (normally one to three verses). The group simply sits, hears the Word, and meditates over it thoughtfully for the remainder of the silence.

2. Share personal experience. One member of the group volunteers to share first. He or she is free to share for up to ten minutes. The sharing can be about whatever is on the friend's mind, with a particular focus on how he or she experienced God during that previous week. The member can talk about external situations that occurred, but the focus should be finding God in the midst of the situation.

3. Actively listen. All other members must focus on listening as the person shares. No one can interrupt with advice or commentary. However, you can respond to what is shared with clarifying responses, such as the following:

- Repeating back what the friend said to ensure you heard everything correctly.
- Asking for more information or clarity if you are having trouble understanding something.
- Don't say anything. Sometimes sitting with them in silence is the best answer.[215]

4. Engage in contemplative prayer. While the friend is sharing, pray silently to Jesus, who is gathered in your midst. Ask him for guidance during the conversation. Be aware of his presence and what he may be up to in the person's life.

5. Ask deep questions. Once the member finishes sharing, the rest of the group can spend up to ten minutes asking questions that guide the member to think spiritually of how God is present in that situation. Again, refrain from giving advice or providing answers at first. See the list of questions at the end of this appendix.

6. Share advice. After the friend sharing has responded to your questions, then the other members of the group can give advice only after verbal agreement from the sharer. The end goal of the groups is not to give advice but to ensure each person is heard. Only give advice if the friend sharing gives you permission.

7. Rotate. Once the first member feels resolved, move to the next member.

8. Pray over each other. Once everyone has shared, conclude the session by praying over each other and what was shared during the session. A helpful approach is to rotate around the circle having each person pray for the person on their left.

9. Determine next session. The leader concludes the session by determining when and where the next session will take place and decides who the next group leader will be.

QUESTION BANK

(Questions inspired by Alice Fryling's *Seeking God Together*, pages 49–53)

QUESTIONS TO GET STARTED

- How has life been for you this last week? What were some high points and low points?
- How has God been present for you in recent weeks? How has God seemed absent?
- What do you think God has been trying to teach you this week?
- What's something you've found yourself longing for recently?

QUESTIONS ABOUT DAILY LIFE

- In what ways has God seemed present in the simple things lately?
- What activities have drawn you closer to God lately? What activities seem to draw you away from God?
- What has been particularly life-giving for you this week?
- What scenarios seem to reveal God's presence to you the most?
- What scenarios seem to shroud God's presence to you the most?

QUESTIONS ABOUT YOUR FAITH JOURNEY

- How have your spiritual practices been lately? (Scripture reading, prayer, worship, etc.)
- What obstacles have been getting in the way of your faith journey and relationship with God recently?
- What has God revealed to you in your Scripture reading lately?
- What are you longing for these days?

QUESTIONS TO ASK ABOUT WHAT THE FRIEND IS SHARING

- How does this situation make you feel?
- How has God been present to you in this situation?

- How do you think God views this situation that you shared?
- How do you think God views you in the midst of this situation?
- How would you like God to come to your aid?
- How is this situation changing the way you view God?
- What are some next steps you believe God might want you to take in light of this discussion?

QUESTIONS TO ASK WHEN DISCUSSION IS AT A STANDSTILL

- Are there any questions you would like us to ask you?
- How can we be the most helpful to you in this situation?

QUESTIONS TO AVOID

- Questions that begin with "why." They can sometimes come across as accusatory or presumptuous.
- Yes-or-no questions that often begin with "Did" and "Do" ("Did you go to God about it?" "Do you think you'll talk to your parents about that?")

APPENDIX B

SPIRITUAL FRIENDSHIP COHORT DATA

My dissertation sought to discover how practicing spiritual friendships could decrease feelings of loneliness and increase a sense of social support among thirty young adults between the ages of eighteen and twenty-four. The following quantitative data compares participants' pre- and post-intervention assessment scores to demonstrate these groups' effectiveness.

CHANGES IN LONELINESS EXPERIENCE

First, my participants completed the UCLA Loneliness Scale Version Three before the study to determine their loneliness experience before and after the ten-week program. I also performed a paired t-test to determine if there was any change in loneliness experience from the pre-intervention assessment scores.

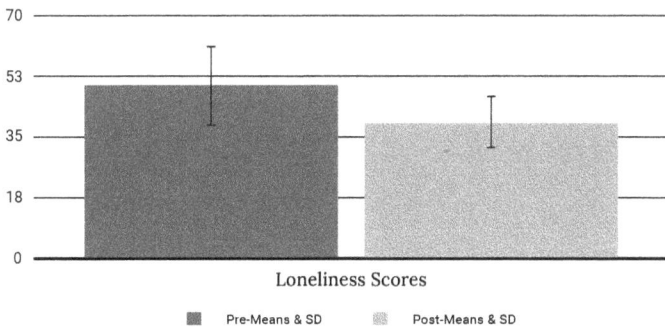

Figure 1: Pre- and Post-Intervention Loneliness Scores

After completing the intervention, the cohort's loneliness score *decreased* from a mean score of 49.66 (out of 80) and a standard deviation of 10.87 to a mean score of 39.34 with a standard deviation of 7.40. The t-test results were (t_{28}=5.404, p < .001, Cohen's d = 10.28), suggesting this was a statistically significant change in loneliness experience.

CHANGES IN SOCIAL SUPPORT

Next, participants completed the Multidimensional Scale of Perceived Social Support before and after the program to measure their sense of social support. In a similar manner, I ran a paired t-test to determine if there were any quantitative changes in their sense of social support.

The mean social support score post-intervention was 5.92 out of 7 with a standard deviation of 0.68. This was significantly higher than the cohort's pre-intervention social support scores (M = 5.43; SD = 1.00; t28 = -4.485, p < .001; Cohen's d = 0.58).

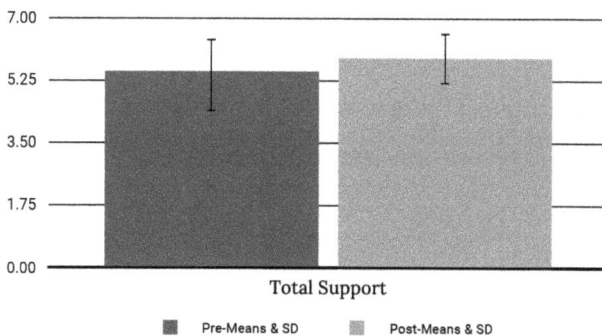

Figure 2: Pre- and Post-Intervention Social Support Scores

There was an increase in all the social support subscales as well. Significant other support increased significantly from (M = 5.92, SD = 1.21) pre-intervention to (M = 6.28, SD = 1.02) post intervention (t29 = -3.00, p = .003, Cohen's d = .67). Family support trended toward increasing from (M = 5.28, SD = 1.42) pre-intervention to (M = 5.50, SD = 1.14) post-intervention (t29 = -1.61, p = .059). Finally, and most notably, friendship support had the most significant increase and the largest effect size of all the subscales, rising from (M = 5.13, SD = 1.07) pre-intervention to (M = 6.01, SD = 0.68) post-intervention (t28 = -4.54, p < .001, Cohen's d = 1.04).

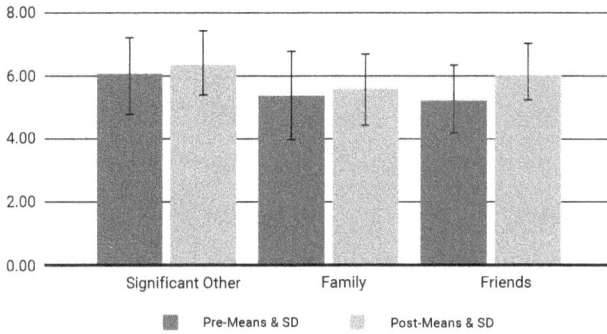

Figure 3: Pre- and Post-Intervention Social Support Subscale Scores

CHANGES IN SPIRITUAL FRIENDSHIP EXPERIENCE

Finally, participants completed the Attitudes, Knowledge, and Experience of Spiritual Friendship Assessment before and after the program to determine the extent of their experience with spiritual friendships. I once again performed a paired t-test to determine if there was any change in spiritual friendship experience after completing the intervention.

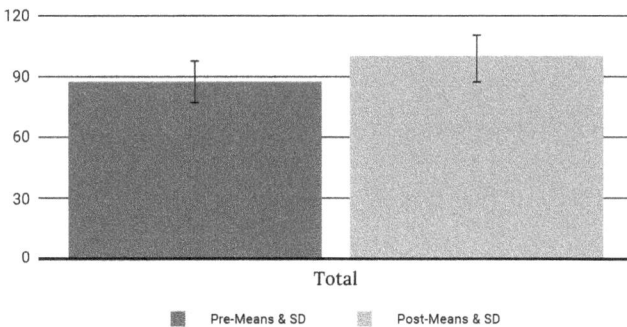

Figure 4: Pre- and Post-Intervention Spiritual Friendship Scores

The mean spiritual friendship score post-intervention was 99.56 out of 120, with a standard deviation of 10.74. This was statistically significantly higher than the cohort's pre-intervention spiritual friendship scores (M = 87.52; SD = 9.89; t26 = -8.112, p < .001, Cohen's d = 7.40) after completing the intervention.

There was a significant increase in all the spiritual friendship subscales as well. Attitudes toward spiritual friendship increased from (M = 32.04, SD = 2.71) pre-intervention to (M = 34.67, SD = 3.58) post intervention (t27 = -4.13, p < .001, Cohen's d = 3.15). Knowledge of spiritual friendship increased from (M = 28.76, SD = 4.64) pre-intervention to (M = 33.13, SD = 3.67) post-intervention (t28 = -7.42, p < .001, Cohen's d = 3.13). Finally, experience with spiritual friendship increased from (M = 26.62, SD = 4.64) pre-intervention to (M = 31.90, SD = 4.35) post-intervention (t27 = -8.29, p < .001, Cohen's d3.26).]

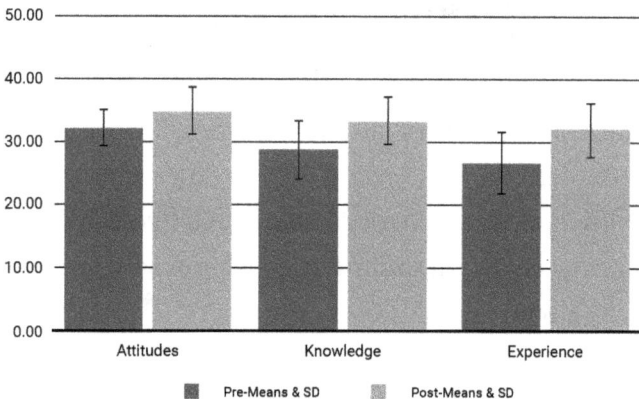

Figure 5: Pre- and Post-Intervention
Spiritual Friendship Subscale Scores

ACKNOWLEDGMENTS

Rarely are major accomplishments achieved in isolation. It took an army of support from my friends, family, and loved ones for this book to become a reality after *ten years*. I want to acknowledge that army.

First and foremost, all praise and glory be to God. This work is devoted to him, as he is the one who has given me this vision and hope for the local church to recover the ancient practice of spiritual friendship for the modern era. Thank you, Jesus, my chief friend.

Second, I could not do this without the support of my wife, Kasey. In fact, what even put me on her radar as a guy she'd consider dating was stumbling upon one of my blogs about spiritual friendship and community all the way back in 2018. She was bought in on the vision of spiritual friendship before we even spoke a word to each other. Thank you, Kasey Jean, for your love and friendship and for pushing me to see my dreams fulfilled. You truly double my life's joys and halve my life's sorrows.

Third, a major thanks to my dear friend Phil Wiseman, my supervisor who gave me a chance as a young, fledgling resident pastor at my first church to teach a four-part summer school class after finishing my master's in 2017. That was the first time I put this work out there for others to hear, and it has only blossomed since then. Thank you for believing in me.

Fourth, to some of my own spiritual friends. Paul and Nate: for your willingness to share our souls together over breakfast at six thirty a.m. on the second Monday of every month. Phill Tague,

David Kinnan, and Dave Bushnell: for your mentorship, guidance, and investment in my life. I wouldn't be the pastor, husband, and person I am without your wise counsel. And to my small group: Jackson, Chelsea, Hannah, Connor, Madi, and Jess! Thank you for your encouragement along the way and for being an incredible batch of Personal-Spiritual friends. Life is sweeter with you by my side.

Fifth, a huge thanks to everyone who made my dissertation possible: the one and only Dr. Andrea Summers, for her incredible mentorship and advising on my project over the course of three years; Drs. Jason Runyan, Paul Garverick, and Patrick Eby, for all your feedback that made the project way better than I could have ever dreamed of; and, most notably, to the thirty young adults who participated in my research.

Sixth, thank you, Resilient Church, the community I have the incredible privilege of ministering to and shepherding. I am so grateful you would even allow me the time to work on this project, let alone guide us all into closer fellowship with one another.

Lastly, thank you to my editor, Deb Hall, for scouring through my manuscript and making this *way better* than I could've imagined! And thank you to the team at SelfPublishing.com and Karen Pina, my author success coach, for all the guidance and expertise you gave me to help me self-publish this work and make my dream a reality.

There are so many more people I could thank, but that would be a book in itself. I am who I am because of the friends the Lord has given me throughout my life, and for that, I couldn't be more grateful.

ABOUT THE AUTHOR

Dr. Jake Thurston is the lead pastor and church planter of Resilient Church, a growing ministry that serves a large number of students and young adults in the college town of Vermillion, South Dakota. He is an adjunct professor of Bible, Theology, and Ministry at Indiana Wesleyan University, Wesley Seminary, and the University of South Dakota. He is married to his wife, Kasey, and has two daughters and one son.

You can follow Jake on Instagram **@pastor.jakethurston**, and join his newsletter at **YouNeedFriends.com**.

JOIN THE NEWSLETTER

Want more content about spiritual friendship and to be kept in the loop about future projects? Head to **YouNeedFriends.com** and join the free newsletter.

ENDNOTES

INTRODUCTION

1 Vivek Murthy, "Work and the Loneliness Epidemic," *Harvard Business Review*, September 26, 2017, https://hbr.org/cover-story/2017/09/work-and-the-loneliness-epidemic.

2 CIGNA, "The Loneliness Epidemic Persists: A Post-Pandemic Look at the State of Loneliness among U.S. Adults," accessed May 2022, https://newsroom.thecignagroup.com/loneliness-epidemic-persists-post-pandemic-look.

3 John Cacioppo, "The Lethality of Loneliness: John Cacioppo at TEDxDesMoines," TedTalk, September 9, 2013, https://www.youtube.com/watch?v=_0hxl03JoA0.

4 I can't put exact years because scholars are all across the board with these age ranges for each generation. Some say Gen Z includes those born between 1995 and 2010, while others say 1997–2012, and still others say 2001–2015.

CHAPTER 1: IT'S NOT GOOD TO BE ALONE

5 Tim Keller, "Spiritual Friendship," sermon, Redeemer Presbyterian Church, March 1, 1998, https://gospelinlife.com/sermon/spiritual-friendship/.

6 John Cacioppo, *Loneliness: Human Nature and the Need for Social Connection* (New York: W. W. Norton and Company, 2008), 127.

7 Carla Perissinotto, "The Health Effects of Loneliness in Our Community," Jewish Community Center of San Francisco, YouTube.com, https://www.youtube.com/watch?v=uYoBXPUDbko.

8 Vivek Murthy, *Together: The Healing Power of Human Connection in a Sometimes Lonely World* (New York: HarperCollins, 2020), 8.

9 John Cacioppo, "The Lethality of Loneliness."

10 Murthy, *Together*, 10–11.

11 Amy Banks, *Wired to Connect: The Surprising Link Between Brain Science and Strong, Healthy Relationships* (New York: Penguin, 2015), 3.

12 Susan Mettes, *The Loneliness Epidemic: Why So Many of Us Feel Alone and How Leaders Can Respond* (Grand Rapids, MI: Brazos Press, 2021), 31–32.

13 Mark Mayfield, *The Path out of Loneliness: Finding and Fostering Connection to God, Ourselves, and One Another* (Colorado Springs, CO: NavPress, 2021), 32.

14 Martin Seligman in Robert D. Putnam, *Bowling Alone: The Collapse and Revival of American Community* (New York: Simon and Schuster, 2000), 261.

15 Mettes, *The Loneliness Epidemic*, 29–30.

16 Murthy, *Together*, 14.

17 Mayfield, *The Path out of Loneliness*, 39.

18 Mayfield, *The Path out of Loneliness*, 43–44.

19 Murthy, *Together*, 11.

20 Henry Cloud, *The Power of the Other: The Startling Effect Other People Have on You, from the Boardroom to the Bedroom and Beyond—and What to Do About It* (New York: HarperCollins, 2016), 44–45.

21 Cloud, *The Power of the Other*, 44–45.

22 Julianna Holt-Lunstad, Timothy B. Smith, and J. Bradley Layton, "Social Relationships and Mortality Risk: A Meta-analytic Review," PLOS *Medicine* 7, no 7 (2010): doi.org/10.1371/journal.pmed.1000316.

23 Mettes, *The Loneliness Epidemic*, 29.

24 David Brooks, *The Second Mountain: The Quest for a Moral Life* (New York: Random House, 2019), 32–33.

25 Justin Whitmel Earley, *Made for People: Why We Drift into Loneliness and How to Fight for a Life of Friendship* (Grand Rapids, MI: Zondervan, 2023), 11.

CHAPTER 2: DESIGNED FOR COMMUNITY

26 Mayfield, *The Path out of Loneliness*, 74.

27 Dennis F. Kinlaw, *Let's Start with Jesus: A New Way of Doing Theology* (Grand Rapids, MI: Zondervan, 2005), 75–79.

28 Kinlaw, *Let's Start with Jesus*, 80.

29 Drew Hunter, *Made for Friendship: The Relationship That Halves Our Sorrows and Doubles Our Joys* (Wheaton, IL: Crossway, 2018), 44.

30 Jonathan Haidt, *The Happiness Hypothesis: Finding Modern Truth in Ancient Wisdom* (New York: Basic Books, 2006), 134.

31 Haidt, *The Happiness Hypothesis*, 134.

32 Haidt, *The Happiness Hypothesis*, 133.

33 Susan Pinker, *The Village Effect: How Face-to-Face Contact Can Make Us Healthier and Happier* (Toronto, Canada: Random House Canada, 2014), Kindle edition, location 127.

34 Robin Dunbar, *Friends: Understanding the Power of Our Most Important Relationships* (London: Little, Brown Book Group, 2022), 4.

35 Dunbar, *Friends*, 6–7.

36 Dunbar, *Friends*, 11.

37 Cacioppo, Loneliness, 137–38, 140.

38 Found in the apocrypha of the Catholic Bible, Sirach 6:16.

39 Haidt, *The Happiness Hypothesis*, 151.

40 Cloud, *The Power of the Other*, 23–24.

41 Dunbar, *Friends*, 8.

42 Banks, *Wired to Connect*, 73–75.

43 Banks, *Wired to Connect*, 79.

44 Banks, *Wired to Connect*, 91, 97.

45 Haidt, *The Happiness Hypothesis*, 219.

46 Murthy, *Together*, 23.

47 Cacioppo, *Loneliness*, 127.

CHAPTER 3: "I DON'T NEED ANYONE ELSE"

48 Joseph H. Hellerman, *When the Church Was a Family: Recapturing Jesus' Vision for Authentic Community* (Nashville: B&H Publishing Group, 2009), 4.

49 Hellerman, *When the Church Was a Family*, 4–5.

50 Mark Lau Branson and Juan F. Martínez, *Churches, Cultures and Leadership* (Downers Grove, IL: InterVarsity Press, 2011), 142–43.

51 Branson and Martínez, *Churches, Cultures, and Leadership*, 155. It should be noted that living in a collectivist culture does not guarantee one never experiences loneliness, just as living in an individualist culture does not automatically induce loneliness. There are issues and benefits with both cultures. In a collectivist society, it is possible for someone to lose sight of his unique individuality due to his constant subservience to the group. He may be connected in more relationships but at the risk of degenerating his sense of self. All the same, America's culture of self-reliance, independence, and a "do-it-yourself" mentality often makes it more difficult for individuals to find communities of meaningful relationships than in collectivist cultures.

52 Hellerman, *When the Church Was a Family*, 4.

53 Andy Root, "Stop Calling Them That," in *Immerse: A Journal of Faith, Life, and Youth Ministry* (Kansas City, MO: 2012), 23.

54 David Kinnaman and Mark Matlock, *Faith for Exiles: 5 Ways for a New Generation to Follow Jesus in Digital Babylon* (Grand Rapids, MI: Baker Publishing, 2019), 47.

55 Tim Elmore, *Generation Z Unfiltered: Facing Nine Hidden Challenges of the Most Anxious Population* (Atlanta: Poet Gardner, 2019), Kindle edition, loc. 3147–50, 3219–35.

56 Randy Frazee, *The Connecting Church 2.0: Beyond Small Groups to Authentic Community*, Scribd e-book ed. (Grand Rapids, MI: Zondervan, 2013), chapter 3.

57 Skye Jethani, *The Divine Commodity: Discovering a Faith Beyond Consumer Christianity* (Grand Rapids, MI: Zondervan, 2009), 126.

58 Christine D. Pohl, *Living into Community: Cultivating Practices That Sustain Us* (Grand Rapids, MI: William B. Eerdmans Publishing, 2012), 78.

59 Pohl, *Living into Community*, 125.

60 Todd Hall, *The Connected Life: The Art and Science of Relational Spirituality* (Downers Grove, IL: InterVarsity Press, 2022), 8–9.

61 Brené Brown, *Braving the Wilderness: The Quest for True Belonging and the Courage to Stand Alone* (New York, NY: Random House, 2019), 53.

62 Natalie Pennington, Jeffrey A. Hall, and Amanda J. Homstrom, "The American Friendship Project: A Report on the Status and Health of Friendship in America," (2024), PLoS ONE 19(7): e0305834, https://doi.org/10.1371/journal.pone.0305834.

63 Pennington, Hall, and Homstrom, "The American Friendship Project."

64 Dunbar, *Friends*, chapter 2.

65 Dunbar, *Friends*, 91–92.

66 "Four Types of Community We All Need (and the Two That Matter Most)," Practicing the Way, YouTube, June 24, 2024, https://www.youtube.com/watch?v=tGOR3leo7Fw.

CHAPTER 4: "I DON'T WANT ANYONE ELSE"

67 Frazee, *The Connecting Church* 2.0, chapter 7.

68 Joseph R. Myers, *The Search to Belong: Rethinking Intimacy, Community, and Small Groups* (Grand Rapids, MI: Zondervan, 2003), chapter 6.

69 Jethani, *The Divine Commodity*, 143.

70 Jethani, *The Divine Commodity*, 143.

71 Simon Sinek, *Leaders Eat Last*, (London: Portfolio, 2014), 266–69.

72 Mettes, *The Loneliness Epidemic*, 51.

73 The stats Haidt gives are very compelling. Depression, mental illness, and anxiety all increased beginning in 2010 and had exploded by 2020. Depression among teens (ages 12–17) saw a 161 percent increase in boys and a 145 percent in teen girls between 2010 and 2020. Among college students, anxiety increased by 134 percent and depression increased by 106 percent between 2010 and 2019. When broken down by age group, ages 50-plus experienced an 8 percent increase in anxiety between 2010 and 2020; ages 35–49 saw a 52 percent increase in anxiety; ages 26–34 saw a 103 percent increase; and ages 18–25 saw a 139 percent increase in anxiety between 2010 and 2020. And these are where these percentages ended in 2020, meaning these numbers were all on the rise well before the COVID-19 pandemic. While COVID certainly proliferated these feelings, it did not cause the increase. Emergency room visits for adolescents aged 10–14 due to self-harm increased in boys by 48 percent between 2010 and 2020, and by 188 percent among girls. After being on a steady decline for a decade, suicide rates among adolescents increased by 91 percent in boys between 2010 and 2020, and 167 percent in girls. See Jonathan Haidt, *The Anxious Generation: How the Great Rewiring of Childhood Is Causing an Epidemic of Mental Illness* (New York: Penguin Random House, 2024), 24–27, 30, 31.

74 Haidt, *The Anxious Generation*, 35–36.

75 Elmore, *Generation Z Unfiltered*, Kindle locations 870, 872, 1075.

76 Tristan Harris, in Haidt, *The Anxious Generation*, 229–30.

77 Kinnaman and Matlock, *Faith for Exiles*, 46–48.

78 Haidt, *The Anxious Generation*, 134–35.

79 Kinnaman and Matlock, *Faith for Exiles*, 26.

80 Jean Twenge, *iGen: Why Today's Super-Connected Kids Are Growing Up Less Rebellious, More Tolerant, Less Happy—and Completely Unprepared for Adulthood, and What That Means for the Rest of Us* (New York: Atria, 2017), 51.

81 Haidt, *The Anxious Generation*, 119.

82 Haidt, *The Anxious Generation*, 54–55.

83 Twenge, *iGen*, 71.

84 Andrew Perrin and Monica Anderson, "Share of U.S. Adults Using Social Media, Including Facebook, Is Mostly Unchanged Since 2018," Pew Research Center, April 10, 2019, https://www.pewresearch.org/fact-tank/2019/04/10/share-of-u-s-adults-using-social-media-including-facebook-is-mostly-unchanged-since-2018.

85 "A third space" is a place for recreation and community outside of one's home and workplace.

86 Kinnaman and Matlock, *Faith for Exiles*, 115.

87 Haidt, *The Anxious Generation*, 169.

88 Dunbar, *Friends*, 84–85.

89 Elmore, *Generation Z Unfiltered*, location 1197.

90 Elmore, *Generation Z Unfiltered*, location, 839.

91 Mayfield, *The Path out of Loneliness*, 52.

92 Mayfield, *The Path out of Loneliness*, 52–53.

93 Mettes, *The Loneliness Epidemic*, 82–83.

94 Elmore, *Generation Z Unfiltered*, location 478.

95 Twenge, *iGen*, 80–81.

96 Haidt, *The Anxious Generation*, 170.

97 Haidt, *The Anxious Generation*, 29.

98 Twenge, *iGen*, 89.

99 Mettes, *The Loneliness Epidemic*, 84.

100 Barna Group, "Teens and Young Adults Use Porn More Than Anyone Else," Barna.

com, January 28, 2016, https://www.barna.com/research/teens-young-adults-use-porn-more-than-anyone-else/.

101 "How Porn Can Affect the Brain Like a Drug," FighttheNewDrug.org, March 21, 2023, https://fightthenewdrug.org/how-porn-can-affect-the-brain-like-a-drug/.

102 M. H. Butler, S. A. Pereyra, T. W. Draper, N. D. Leonhardt, and K. B. Skinner, "Pornography Use and Loneliness: A Bidirectional Recursive Model and Pilot Investigation, Journal of Sex and Marital Therapy" (2018), 44:2, 127–37, doi: 10.1080/0092623X.2017.1321601.

103 "How Porn Can Impact Mental Health and Fuel Loneliness," FighttheNewDrug.org, March 21, 2023, https://fightthenewdrug.org/how-porn-can-impact-mental-health-and-fuel-loneliness/.

104 Haidt, *The Anxious Generation*, 122.

105 Mettes, *The Loneliness Epidemic*, 52.

CHAPTER 5: JESUS IS A FRIEND OF YOURS

106 Brian Edgar, *God Is Friendship: A Theology of Spirituality, Community, and Society* (Wilmore, KY: Seedbed Publishing, 2013), 20.

107 Edgar, *God Is Friendship*, 20–22.

108 Edgar, *God Is Friendship*, 50.

109 Edgar, *God Is Friendship*, 18–19.

110 Dr. Todd Hall talks about how trauma in our relationships, especially within our important attachment relationships like with a parent or guardian, highly influence how we view and relate with God. See Hall, *The Connected Life*, 96.

111 Edgar, *God Is Friendship*, 22–23.

112 Edgar, *God Is Friendship*, 37–39.

113 Jürgen Moltmann, *The Church in the Power of the Spirit*, trans. Margaret Kohl (New York: Harper and Row, 1977), 316.

114 Edgar, *God Is Friendship*, 170.

115 Edgar, *God Is Friendship*, 20.

116 Edgar, *God Is Friendship*, 29.

CHAPTER 6: FRIENDSHIP AS FORMATION

117 John Mark Comer, *Practicing the Way: Be with Jesus. Become like him. Do as he did.* (Colorado Springs, CO: Waterbrook, 2024), 98.

118 Dennis Billy, *Spiritual Friendship: The Classic Text with a Spiritual Commentary* (Notre Dame, IN: Ave Maria Press, 2008), 2–3.

119 Billy, *Spiritual Friendship*, 3–4.

120 Billy, *Spiritual Friendship*, 5–7.

121 Aelred of Rievaulx, *Spiritual Friendship*, bk. II, para. 9. Aelred's optimism toward friendship was rather unorthodox. His stance on friendship was held by only a minority of monastics at the time. Many monastic traditions following him wrote off friendship as a viable means to spiritual formation due to the fear of cliques and disrupting the community through the inevitable strife of human relationships. This unfortunately led to the disregard of spiritual friendship for almost a millennium (see Edgar, *God Is Friendship*, 81). However, a reconsideration of Aelred's work is of utmost importance for a culture yearning for deeper spiritual formation.

122 Although Aelred's discussion of the three types of friendship is primarily found in Book One of his treatise, many of his other guidelines, qualities, and descriptions of friendship can be sorted into these three categories.

123 Aelred, *Spiritual Friendship*, bk. I, para. 38.

124 Aelred, *Spiritual Friendship*, bk. I, para. 39–41.

125 Cloud, *The Power of the Other*, 40–41.

126 Edgar, *God Is Friendship*, 103.

127 Aelred, *Spiritual Friendship*, bk. II, para. 55.

128 Aelred, *Spiritual Friendship*, bk. II, para. 38–39.

129 Aelred, *Spiritual Friendship*, bk. I, para. 42–43.

130 Edgar, *God Is Friendship*, 104–5.

131 Aelred, *Spiritual Friendship*, bk. I, para. 44.

132 Edgar, *God Is Friendship*, 111–12.

133 Edgar, *God Is Friendship*, 115–16.

134 Kelly Needham, *Friendish: Reclaiming Real Friendship in a Culture of Confusion* (Nashville: Nelson Books, 2019), 12–17, 19–34.

135 Aelred, *Spiritual Friendship*, bk. I, para. 69.

136 David G. Benner, *Sacred Companions: The Gift of Spiritual Friendship and Direction* (Downers Grove, IL: InterVarsity Press, 2002) 41, 57.

137 Aelred, *Spiritual Friendship*, bk. I, para. 1.

138 Edgar, *God Is Friendship*, 77.

139 Banks, *Wired to Connect*, 91, 97.

140 Daniel J. Siegel and Tina Payne Bryson, *The Whole-Brain Child* (New York: Bantam Books, 2012), 122.

141 See Edgar, *God Is Friendship*, 73–77.

142 Aelred, *Spiritual Friendship*, bk. I, para. 45–49.

143 Edgar, *God Is Friendship*, 77.

144 Aelred, *Spiritual Friendship*, bk. II, para. 11–12.

CHAPTER 7: WHOM SHOULD YOU BEFRIEND?

145 See Joseph R. Myers' book *The Search to Belong* for a deep dive into the four spaces and how to apply them to belonging in the local church.

146 Banks, *Wired to Connect*, 73–81.

147 Banks, *Wired to Connect*, 91, 97.

148 Edgar, *God Is Friendship*, 103.

149 Aelred, Spiritual Friendship, bk. III, para. 14.

CHAPTER 8: THE BROTHERS AND SISTERS YOU DIDN'T KNOW YOU HAD

150 Thomas Parkinson, *The Loneliness Epidemic: How the Church Can Cure Our Gravest Sickness* (pub. by author, 2021), 22.

151 Pew Research Center, "In U.S., Decline of Christianity Continues at Rapid Pace," October 17, 2019, https://www.pewforum.org/2019/10/17/in-u-s-decline-of-christianity-continues-at-rapid-pace/.

152 Mettes, *The Loneliness Epidemic*, 95–96.

153 Parkinson, *The Loneliness Epidemic*, 4–5.

154 Twenge, *iGen*, 128.

155 Barna Group, *Gen Z: The Culture, Beliefs, and Motivations Shaping the Next Generation* (Ventura, CA: Barna Group and Impact 360 Institute, 2018), 25.

156 James Emery White, *Meet Generation Z: Understanding and Reaching the New Post-Christian World* (Grand Rapids, MI: BakerBooks, 2017), 49.

157 Twenge, *iGen*, 121, 124–5. Some argue that it is normal for young people to be less religiously affiliated during their independent years, who will later return to church or religion when they settle down and have a family. While this is true in some cases, it is happening at a lesser rate for Millennials than it did for previous generations, "making it unlikely that [Gen Zers] will either."

158 Barna Group, *Gen Z*, 26.

159 Twenge, *iGen*, 138.

160 Twenge, *iGen*, 139. This especially applies toward those who belong to the LGBTQ+ community, to which nearly 20 percent of Gen Zers say they belong.

161 Elmore, *Generation Z Unfiltered*, location 3152.

162 Barna Group, *Gen Z*, 64–65.

163 Comer, *Practicing the Way*, 187.

164 Hellerman, *When the Church Was a Family*, 205–15.

165 Hellerman, *When the Church Was a Family*, 124.

166 Hellerman, *When the Church Was a Family*, 124.

167 Hellerman, *When the Church Was a Family*, 136.

168 Kinnaman and Matlock, *Faith for Exiles*, 113.

CHAPTER 9: NAKED AND UNASHAMED

169 Earley, *Made for People*, 16, 17.

170 Brené Brown, *Daring Greatly: How the Courage to Be Vulnerable Transforms the Way We Live, Love, Parent, and Lead* (New York: Penguin Random House, 2012), 69.

171 Brown, *Daring Greatly*, 68.

172 Brown, *Daring Greatly*, 71, 73, 77.

173 Dietrich Bonhoeffer, *Life Together: The Classic Exploration of Christian Community*, trans. John W. Doberstein (New York: HarperOne, 1954), 110.

174 Brown, *Daring Greatly*, 67–68.

175 Bonhoeffer, *Life Together*, 26–27.

176 Brown, *Daring Greatly*, 33.

177 Richard Foster, *The Celebration of Discipline* (New York: HarperCollins, 1998), 145.

178 Bonhoeffer, *Life Together*, 27.

179 Earley, *Made for People*, 43.

180 Brown, *Daring Greatly*, 34.

181 Brown, *Daring Greatly*, 75.

182 Hall, *The Connected Life*, 105.

183 Earley, *Made for People*, 25.

184 Brown, *Daring Greatly*, 82.

185 Hall, *The Connected Life*, 180–81.

186 Aelred, *Spiritual Friendship*, bk. III, para. 133.

187 Ruth Haley Barton, *Life Together in Christian Community: Experiencing Transformation in Community* (Downers Grove, IL: InterVarsity Press, 2014), 75–76.

188 Benner, *Sacred Companions*, 74.

189 Barton, *Life Together in Christian Community*, 79.

190 Earley, *Made for Friendship*, 54.

191 Benner, *Sacred Companions*, 73.

192 Bonhoeffer, *Life Together*, 112–13.

193 Bonhoeffer, *Life Together*, 112–13.

194 Earley, *Made for People*, 47.

195 Earley, *Made for People*, 14.

CHAPTER 10: HOW IS IT WITH YOUR SOUL?

196 Kevin Watson, "The Small Group Band Meeting: A Place to Grow in Holiness Together," Seedbed, January 27, 2016, https://seedbed.com/the-small-group-band-a-place-to-grow-in-holiness-together/.

197 Barton, *Life Together in Christian Community*, 10–11.

198 Benner, *Sacred Companions*, 165–66.

199 Alice Fryling, *Seeking God Together: An Introduction to Group Spiritual Direction* (Downers Grove, IL: InterVarsity Press, 2009), 11.

200 Fryling, *Seeking God Together*, 11–13, 20, 26.

201 Fryling, *Seeking God Together*, 29.

202 Fryling, *Seeking God Together*, 21–22.

203 Benner, *Sacred Companions*, 173.

204 Fryling, *Seeking God Together*, 41.

205 Benner, *Sacred Companions*, 172–73.

206 Bonhoeffer, *Life Together*, 97.

207 Fryling, *Seeking God Together*, 40.

208 Benner, Sacred Companions, 168–71.

209 Fryling, *Seeking God Together*, 20.

210 Fryling, *Seeking God Together*, 45.

211 Benner, *Sacred Companions*, 167–68.

212 Benner, *Sacred Companions*, 174, 176.

213 Benner, *Sacred Companions*, 177.

CONCLUSION

214 *The Lord of the Rings: The Return of the King*, directed by Peter Jackson (2003: New Line Cinema), 2:34:34.

APPENDIX A

215 Fryling, *Seeking God Together*, 42–43.

NOTES